Island

JOURNEYS

JOURNEYS

The Impact of the Island Way of Life
at Home and Abroad

CARLISLE RICHARDSON

Published by Advantage, Charleston, South Carolina.
Member of Advantage Media Group.

ADVANTAGE is a registered trademark and the Advantage colophon is a trademark of Advantage Media Group, Inc.

Printed in the United States of America.

ISBN: 978-1-59932-612-2
LCCN: 2015942540

This publication is designed to provide accurate and authoritative information in regard to the subject matter covered. It is sold with the understanding that the publisher is not engaged in rendering legal, accounting, or other professional services. If legal advice or other expert assistance is required, the services of a competent professional person should be sought.

Advantage Media Group is proud to be a part of the Tree Neutral® program. Tree Neutral offsets the number of trees consumed in the production and printing of this book by taking proactive steps such as planting trees in direct proportion to the number of trees used to print books. To learn more about Tree Neutral, please visit **www.treeneutral.com**. To learn more about Advantage's commitment to being a responsible steward of the environment, please visit **www.advantagefamily.com/green**

Advantage Media Group is a publisher of business, self-improvement, and professional development books and online learning. We help entrepreneurs, business leaders, and professionals share their Stories, Passion, and Knowledge to help others Learn & Grow. Do you have a manuscript or book idea that you would like us to consider for publishing? Please visit **advantagefamily.com** or call **1.866.775.1696.**

*To my parents, who chose to remain in the islands and showed
me just how beautiful and amazing they are.*

*To my siblings, who understood so much about this journey
and encouraged me for years to embark on it.*

*To my wife, who provided unconditional support and understanding,
particularly as I made each trip.*

*And to my daughter, who represents the next generation of islanders.
May you grow to love them as much as I do.*

Disclaimer

The views expressed in this publication are not intended to reflect or represent the views and position of the government of St. Kitts and Nevis or the United Nations. They represent the views of the author or the individuals referred to in the book.

ACKNOWLEDGMENTS

There have been many people who have played an important part in the realization of my island journeys: family, friends, classmates, flatmates, coworkers, colleagues, and acquaintances all. To you I say, "Thank you for helping me to mature to this point."

I need to single out a few who were instrumental in my writing and publishing *Island Journeys*. I want to especially thank

> Dr. Leonard Richardson, who helped me to focus on what I wanted to say and share with the world;
>
> Sally Richardson, Marissa Richardson, Sherri Chambers, Qais Yousef, and Isabelle Mckusick, for the photos you provided. They helped bring the stories to life;
>
> Edwin Perez, for introducing me to the culture of the Dominican Republic while you and your daughters gave me a tour of Washington Heights;
>
> Stephanie Rambler, for allowing me to bounce some of these ideas off you for your feedback, while we embarked on the trips to Jamaica, Fiji, Seychelles and Samoa. You understand the islands and have become a true islander yourself. Also, you have many wonderful stories of your own that I hope you share with the world one day;

Diane Quarless, for being instrumental in guiding my island journey and being my mentor, both as a delegate and at the UN. You know better than I do the story of the islands;

and the team at Advantage Media Group, who made all of this possible by helping me to dig deeper and bring out the best for this book.

Thank you all for embarking on this journey with me.

ABOUT THE AUTHOR

Carlisle Richardson was born in St. Kitts and Nevis in the Caribbean. He was educated at the primary and secondary levels in St. Kitts and pursued his higher education at the University of the West Indies in Barbados where he graduated with honors with a BS in economics and history, and in Trinidad and Tobago, where he completed a postgraduate diploma in international relations. He gained his master's degree in international relations at the University of Sussex in the United Kingdom. His master's degree thesis was titled "The Development Agenda of the UN General Assembly in the Post-Cold War Era: A Break from the Past?" and included a focus study on small island developing states (SIDS).

Mr. Richardson joined the service of the Ministry of Foreign Affairs of St. Kitts and Nevis and was posted to the Permanent Mission of St. Kitts and Nevis to the United Nations (UN) in 2001. He was lead negotiator for St. Kitts and Nevis at the UN during the preparatory process of the International Meeting on Small Island Developing States held in Mauritius in 2005. Additionally, during his tenure at the Permanent Mission to the UN, Mr. Richardson drafted the statements of St. Kitts and Nevis to the high-level general debates of the UN General Assembly and was one of the first representatives of St. Kitts and Nevis ever to address the UN Economic and Social Council in Geneva.

In 2011, Mr. Richardson joined the UN and worked in the Division for Sustainable Development where he was a key figure in the work on small island developing states issues for the 2012 UN Conference on Sustainable Development (Rio+20). Additionally, at the SIDS Unit of the Division for Sustainable Development, he was part of the team that prepared for and organized the Third International Conference on Small Island Developing States, held in Samoa in 2014. He drafted many of the statements of the Conference Secretary General and other high-level officials of the UN in preparation for the conference. He also drafted several UN reports on the sustainable development of small island developing states.

Mr. Richardson wrote the article "Punching above Our Weight: Representing St. Kitts and Nevis in the International Arena," which was featured in the *St. Kitts and Nevis 25th Independence Anniversary Magazine* in 2008.

It is his intention to establish the Island Foundation, which will be dedicated to promoting education, the arts, sports, and innovation on islands, while preserving island culture and heritage.

The Spark for an Island Book

We could see the orange haze of fire in the distance, but we ourselves were surrounded by darkness. The silhouette of the mountain in the expanse beyond the plains seemed ominous. It told the tale of many souls that had the misfortune of losing their way.

Every scary story we had heard as children, whenever there had been a power outage, found its way to my mind. I tried willing each one of them away, but the more I tried and the less hopeful the van sounded, the more intensified was my imagination of an unpromising end.

"We have to make the summit," I finally forced myself to think.

The van lurched forward, and all its passengers held their collective breath, while the driver kept her eyes ahead. She had already pulled out her cell phone, prepared to make that emergency call if necessary. Would they get to us in time? We could only hope.

The van struggled on. It sputtered once more, and again, we held our collective breath. The driver pressed down completely on the gas. This was it, the deciding moment.

Finally, the gear kicked in, and we surged forward.

The transmission strained but held. You could hear the wail, but we were still moving. The top of the hill was in sight, and the incline started to ease. The van picked up speed, and finally, we were at the top, looking down at the city in the distance. We did not have to get out and push. We could breathe again.

Three bush fires stood between us and the city, but it was all downhill. We would put foot to metal, brace for it, and go.

It was at this moment I realized *that* was what it meant to be an islander. Whether it's my native St. Kitts and Nevis or Samoa, Seychelles, or Fiji, living in an "island paradise" offers stunning beauty but also extreme challenges and dangers that outsiders may never know exist.

I grew up on an island, and though I was racing in a van through bush fires to board a plane to leave another island, I couldn't stop thinking that non-islanders needed to know there was so much more to island life than beaches and resorts. Barreling down the hillside past the smoking tree line rekindled a passion in me to share not just my island stories but *the* island story.

As suddenly as the crisis had started, it was over. The driver was a gem; she navigated the van like a veteran and pushed through to safety. Twenty minutes later, we were running to catch our flight in the nick of time, and the spark for this book was kindled and blazing.

I was thrilled to be one of the organizers of the Third International Conference on Small Island Developing States held in Samoa in 2014. The experience opened my eyes in new ways. Throughout my life, I had often felt a kinship with other islanders. Now, surrounded by delegates from isolated dots on the map that were just as difficult to find as my island was in comparison with massive continental powers, I felt a new sense of pride.

In Samoa, and as I continued to travel the islands, the experience of the conference allowed me to reflect on who we islanders are: men and women who have an impact not only on our island homes but on the larger countries as well. Some of us are members of the diaspora. Working within our former colonial powers, we form a disproportionately large percentage of the native populations of our homelands. Others have rarely left our islands, finding strength in the challenges at home and using our education and experiences to better the situation for ourselves and all the others who remain to continue building the islands into better, more modern places. All of us are finding ways to connect with an increasingly globalized world and still maintain our culture—always a tricky balance.

I found that no matter what distant archipelago I found myself on, I would always feel at home. It did not matter the languages the locals spoke, the plants that grew from the beaches and spread through to the highest mountaintops, or the structure of the economy. I would find that each of these island chains, whether in the Caribbean, the Indian Ocean, the Pacific, or other seas, all shared physical, cultural, and social traits with which I had grown up. Each would welcome me as a native son, and I would find I shared bonds that enabled me to immediately become part of the place's eternal rhythms and understand the locals.

Indeed, my experience preparing for the Samoa conference and being in Samoa changed me. It strengthened me. It allowed me to understand more of myself and others like me who had grown up on islands.

This epiphany triggered within me a desire to share my experiences and parse out the broad themes from the conference and my own travels to show how much we islanders have a common bond. Over the past 15 years, I have traveled to many islands of the world, as a tourist, as an island delegate attending meetings and conferences on island affairs, and as a UN employee working on small island developing states issues. Now, in this book, I wanted to take those experiences and analyze them, first, of course, for my brothers and sisters raised, as I was, to understand our commonalities. Just as importantly, though, I wanted to do it to share my knowledge of the complexities of the island social environment with those of you not familiar with island life beyond the all-inclusive hotel or vacation brochure.

This is not a guidebook in the traditional sense. Certainly, you'll learn about the natural wonders I witnessed, the markets I purchased souvenirs in, and the restaurants where I tasted local delicacies. But my story isn't about names and places. It's about my experiences; the people I met; and, importantly, all the social, economic, and cultural forces, mixes, and upheavals that led to the creation of the particular locale in which I am making my observations.

I hope international readers will find much to delight them, especially if my writing helps them better understand their own experiences in these far-flung islands across the globe. I also hope readers from the islands will nod their heads vigorously, shouting, "Yes!" as they hit certain pages, understanding the commonalities we all share as islanders.

We will visit Samoa for the conference and to understand its natural wonders, along with Fiji, the Seychelles, Jamaica, and, of course, my native St. Kitts and Nevis. The book also looks at the impact of islanders in places as diverse as London, New York, and even Qatar in the Middle East where Caribbean icons such as Bob Marley connected me, in taxi cab rides, to my native lands and allowed deep, meaningful conversations with the locals, even when I clearly stood out as a stranger among them.

Throughout the book, I explore many themes that have arisen from my travels. Among them is the occasional lack of appreciation and, at times, even shame, when we islanders think of our native lands, especially when comparing ourselves to the great powers. At the same time, we islanders love and look to the outside world. Our common bonds of coming together as communities are also explored. You'll see this expressed when natural forces such as hurricanes are against us, but it is also evident in the international sports world, especially when our beloved cricket teams are competing. Television screens across the globe reunite us in victory—and in defeat.

In this book, we will begin the journey together. And just as that courageous, resourceful driver did on that van trip that so sparked my imagination, I will drive and guide you. We will sometimes find ourselves sputtering, sometimes struck in awe and wonder, but always together as new friends in this island world, understanding our common bonds.

FOREWORD

Writing books is not a hotly sought after occupation by islanders, so I was extremely proud that Carlisle, a true islander, has stepped outside of our traditional comfort zone to tell our "island journeys" through life's uncharted waters. His perspective offers the outside world a rare glimpse at why, as the song says, "you can take the boy from the island but not the island from the boy."

When it comes to the global stage, islanders are rarely understood and selectively appreciated; Carlisle's book will help to bring down some of these walls of ignorance. I particularly like how he uses his experience growing up in the islands as the central point of reference against which he sees the wider world around him. As he becomes a globetrotter and a pacesetter in his own right, Carlisle is able to make the connections between the islands and the world through his heartwarming tales.

In more ways than one, Carlisle's journey is the journey of every islander who has left the comfort of home and the family support system to venture out in search of that illusive paradise. The book gives islanders all over the world a way to reminisce, value, and appreciate some of the islands' unique peculiarities as well as a sense of pride in their individual and collective contributions in all walks of life. And islanders have a high resilience with and endless capacity to adapt to any new surrounding they find themselves in and call them "their home away from home."

There are definite parallels between Carlisle's journey and my own. I am Samoan, a product of our Pacific regional university in Fiji, an officer of our Foreign Service, and I have been away from home intermittently for many years. Having been with our Permanent Mission to the United Nations for some years now, I have been a temporary New Yorker. I have also been involved in the preparations for the Third International Conference of Small Island Developing States, and I have witnessed the work Carlisle and his colleagues did to make the conference a success.

Carlisle has indeed raised the bar high for other islanders to aspire to, and I wish him continued success on his never-ending journey in life.

Ma lo'u fa'aaloalo lava,

—H.E. Ali'ioaiga Feturi Elisaia
Ambassador Extraordinary and Plenipotentiary
Permanent Representative of Samoa to the United Nations

TABLE OF CONTENTS

INTRODUCTION

What Makes Islanders Tick

Islet in Samoa.

C oming from a small island developing state, a term used by
the international community to describe countries like mine,
I have often reflected on islanders' varying sentiments about their
place of birth. Some never want to leave the shores within which they
were born, while others cannot wait to leave, almost embarrassed
about where they were sired.

Many islanders share a feeling of contentment with life in their island home before they become aware of the outside world. They have a wide variety of fruit trees that can satisfy any discriminating palate, and their beaches provide countless hours of enjoyment for islanders of all ages. The family network all across the land means that the socialization process extends beyond their neighborhood, and the parties can last until morning when the sun rises over the sandy shores.

However, when we islanders become aware of the outside world, much as Plato's Allegory of the Cave describes, our perception changes. We suddenly feel the limits of our surroundings, and we want more than what we have. It is at this point that the two extremes kick in. There are those who want to preserve the island existence and fear any disturbances that may upset the balance, and there are others who feel the walls closing in when the elements of the outside world seem so much more attractive than their island world.

These extreme sentiments—which are not the only ones islanders have; many of us love our island homes, even if we do move away from time to time—are, to a large extent, determined by external factors that either bring fear of losing the innocence of the island or the shame of being from an island, far away from the ruling corners of the world.

So what are the external factors that elicit such an internal response? How does the outside world perceive island life?

Tropical islands have sometimes been viewed as locales of escapism, exotic destinations where mouthwatering cuisines and addictive festivals merge in one kaleidoscope of excitement surrounded by beautiful beaches. They have been seen by many for a long time as a source of relaxation, sand, sun, and fun: the perfect place to vacation, or retire to, once the hectic life of the metropolitan world has taken its toll. From these perspectives, then, islands are a good thing. But such views give tropical islands an almost *illusory* appeal, paradises for a brief respite, and then, back to reality.

What about those who have no illusions, those who do not see tropical islands as paradise? Some view them as places where money laundering is possible and where shady characters can disappear from law enforcement officers hunting them around the world. Such a view creates an image of greed and corruption, of islands where wealthy business people can travel and exploit the local situation.

Others are indifferent to islands, viewing them as not accounting for much in the broader scheme of things. It delights me when we islanders prove them wrong, but those beliefs remain.

I remember traveling to a Middle Eastern country, Qatar, in 2005, where the name of my country was so obscure at the time that it was not even a choice in that country's customs and passport control system. The Qatar immigration officers were, at least, apologetic. Others have not been so nice, as if I had simply completely forged my passport, my nation, my very existence. However, because my Qatar trip was one of my first experiences of this kind, it was a sting I will never forget.

I later met a Chinese national who also had never heard of my island. He too apologized and asked many questions to learn more. He was amazed when he learned the size of the population of St. Kitts and Nevis, my home, and tried to put it in the context of the population of China. He couldn't. The population of my islands might not even equal the size of a Beijing city block population.

The reality is that the Super Bowl venues in North America, the soccer arenas throughout Europe, or the cricket stadiums in Australia and New Zealand hold more people than the population of many of the smaller islands. These include my own, the population of which numbers just above 50,000 residents. For all those trying to wrap their mind around our size, it is a challenge. I have even been asked if I know everyone on the island. It is simply assumed that all we islanders know each other.

One day, my niece, a true sweetheart, wanted to know where on the map we were living. When she was shown the area where we should be, she started crying because the map showed only water. Our island was not on the map, so she assumed we must be loose in the ocean, a difficult concept for a three-year-old to reconcile.

Whenever I see a map of the world, I check not only for my island but for all of the others. If they are not there, I try to amicably bring this across: can't have my niece crying. I remember some very nice ladies who worked in a department store in the seaside resort of Brighton, England. They helped me to find a map that showed most of the islands so that I could point out my island to my fellow students at the University of Sussex. It was good to know that others understood.

One of my most unfortunate encounters was with someone who kept referring to the "social instability" of islands. This person boldly announced that some of our cities were the most violent on the planet and that our young people could not wait to flee these places for a better life outside.

Initially, this exchange made me angry, but truly, the dominant emotion for me was disappointment that someone thought this of us. I have traveled to many islands, and I have lived on a few. I have many friends who are from islands, and I myself have very fond memories of being raised on an island. I have never seen social instability on any of them. I knew that she had visited some islands, and from what I had learned, she actually never had a threatening moment on any of them. Rather, the islanders had made her stay quite enjoyable, yet this was her opinion.

Where did this belief come from? Why such a view? The social challenges of islands are the social challenges affecting the world, yet this had not been considered by this person.

There has been much dialogue on the environmental and economic challenges islands face, which was also a major focus of the Samoa conference. Still, I have always felt more needed to be said about the social aspect of islands. Perhaps, if more were said on this topic, such a negative sentiment, which this woman reflected, would cease to exist.

The social element is the lifeblood of a people, and islands have rich interconnected societies that function as extended families. It is these societies that face hurricanes, floods and typhoons, climate change, sea level rise, and external shocks that have an impact on everyone on the island. Yet these societies remain resilient and try to preserve their heritage. If there is any instability, it is due to economic and environmental shocks, but islands do not usually suffer from social instability.

The most telling example of outside sentiment can, perhaps, be summed up in Jon Stewart's monologue on *The Daily Show*. On September 29, 2014, he spoke of the UN Climate Summit and feigned confusion over the term *SIDS*. As it relates to islands, SIDS means small island developing states, but Stewart joked, "Talk about people who can't catch a break. They even have to share their acronym with sudden infant death syndrome."[1]

1Stewart, Jon, "The Warm Ultimatum," *The Daily Show* (Comedy Central, Viacom Media Networks, September 29, 2014.)

Now, I love Jon Stewart's wit, and I appreciate what he meant in his monologue on the plight of islands challenged by climate change. Still, it does underscore part of the problem. The plight of islands is given a passing reference within the broader global context, even on matters that affect them most. Their issues are relegated to secondary status.

I would never suggest that islands are more important than anywhere or anything else. I also understand that larger areas with bigger populations may generate more interest simply because of their size. But islands do matter, and they matter significantly. In fact, because of their size, they sometimes need a little extra attention.

There is so much more to islands and their people than a peripheral glance or minor conversation. There are truly dynamic and fascinating tales to be told.

To understand the peoples of this planet and empathize with their issues, it is good to share experiences with them. Nonchalance would cease to exist with a more intimate comprehension of the historic struggles that people have faced and the challenges they currently face. When island nations march with their flags at the Olympic Games, for example, an educated public would appreciate what it took for these often tiny contingents, sometimes one or two people, to be there. As they march next to big teams from the great powers, an informed public would cheer with them and promote these island nations' stories to the networks.

Islanders are very family oriented, and sharing experiences with them makes you family. You can never fully turn your back on family, can you?

With this in mind, I decided to share some of the experiences of my island journeys over the past 15 years, trips conducted for pleasure, business, and for official duties to introduce and welcome all to the island way of life.

So who, then, are we islanders? What makes us tick? What makes us laugh and cry? What inspires us?

With every journey of exploration and understanding, you have to begin at home, and so I started my consideration of these questions in the Caribbean.

Chapter 1

HOW MY CARIBBEAN HOMELAND SHAPED ME

Charlestown, Nevis. (Photo courtesy of Sally Richardson.)

The Caribbean was not my first love I am sad to confess. I was among those who wanted to leave. Growing up, thanks to the rise of media programming and advertising from the outside world, I felt a very strong pull.

I remember going, one day, to class in primary school, and a classmate brought an apple to eat during recess. Apples don't grow in the Caribbean, and this would have been the first time many of us had seen this "exotic" fruit. It was the beginning of the opening of our island's economy to these unusual imports. We salivated as she bit into this red, bulbous thing. Suddenly, our local fruits, which we could eat at any given moment, were not so appealing.

It was tragic, I know, but so very real in our young, impressionable minds. I suppose it's no accident that all these years later, many of the local fruits at home are not as available as they once were when I was young. If we don't value and nurture our local fruits, they can't survive. I long for them now: guavas, tamarind, pomserettes (called dunks in other islands, they resemble small green apples), sugar apples (also called sweet sop, a white, creamy-fleshed, syrupy fruit), and the like. I know they are around, but they are harder and harder to find.

Sometimes, during summer vacations, we got to travel but not to other Caribbean islands. Many West Indians, at that time, visited North America or Europe, not because of a lack of interest in the other islands, but rather, because most West Indians have family in North America and Europe. Also, and this is sad, it was sometimes cheaper to travel to Miami or New York than to embark on inter-regional travel. I think that has now changed to an extent, but the problem rears its head every so often.

So when the time came for university, I wanted to go to North America or Europe. That world was exciting to me. I had visited abroad and seen enough shows on television to believe I could better identify with this world than my own.

I suspect my parents sensed I was losing my Caribbean-ness, and they brought their alma mater, the University of the West Indies (UWI), into the mix. UWI has campuses on various islands in the Caribbean, and some of them follow a similar syllabus and ideology.

My parents were not partial to any particular campus; they just wanted me to have the UWI experience. I fought it. I did. I used every possible argument I could conceive to go elsewhere, but they knew better. I would be educated about my own realities first before I ventured into the world.

So my Caribbean love began there. It was at UWI that I came to understand and appreciate what it meant to be from the Caribbean. This not only came from the lectures but from living among other Caribbean nationals.

I became an expert in picking up the different nuances of the other islanders even before they spoke. For example, people from Trinidad and Tobago walk as though they have a song playing in their heads all the time.

I first studied at the UWI Cave Hill campus in Barbados. At that time, during the first semester of each academic year, as part of the extracurricular activities, we focused on the culture of different islands each week, culminating in an Island Night on the weekend at which we sampled the food, enjoyed cultural performances, and had a party featuring the music of the island we were celebrating. It was here that I developed a true desire for guava duff from the Bahamas, a dessert made from fruit folded into dough, and oil down from Grenada, a one pot meal of meats, breadfruit, and other ingredients.

Suddenly, this was all that mattered. My Caribbean love was complete. It didn't take long.

I found that our shared Caribbean history is filled with numerous triumphs over adversity, contributions to the international community, and cross-generational inspirations. I felt I was part of something special and would take this feeling with me wherever I roamed. This pride would never be extinguished. I thank my parents for this. They helped me to find my identity. The Caribbean islands helped to define me and prepare me for a deeper exploration of islands the world over.

Understanding all of this about my roots, the Caribbean moments became more pronounced within me. Once I recognized how those early experiences had shaped me to be the man I am today, the memories of them became indelible.

Rally Round the West Indies

One of my most vivid Caribbean memories took place when I was studying in Barbados. At that time, every year, after the end of the carnival in Trinidad and Tobago, the most popular performers from there would visit Barbados for a show with the most popular Barbadian performers. This event was known as the Calypso Spectacular, and it was a truly enthralling performance for carnival revelers, especially those who could not visit Trinidad itself for that year's carnival.

In 1996 the Calypso Spectacular took place on Saturday, March 16, two days after the semifinal Cricket World Cup match between the West Indies and Australia.

Cricket was once king in the Caribbean. Once upon a time, no schoolboy could wait for recess, when he would show his skills as a bowler or master batsman. In high school, there were girls' cricket matches, which started to rival the boys' games. The West Indies cricket team once dominated the sport throughout the world, and it was a source of pride to all West Indians. When the first Cricket World Cup was played at Lord's in London in 1975, the West Indies won. The team repeated this in 1979 and was the runner up in 1983.

Everyone expected our team to win again very soon, but it didn't. In 1996, all indications were that we could finally pull this one off. We had, on the West Indies team at that time, the reigning record holder for runs scored and also some of the most feared bowlers ever to play the game. How could we lose?

That was the first Cricket World Cup match in which I had a vested interest; I was too young to remember most of the others. It was to be our return to the finals and victory. Australia had a very good team, but we were prepared. I woke up very early that morning to watch the match on television as it was taking place in India.

Australia batted first and made 207 runs off eight wickets in 50 overs. We had this. We knew we could win. Our batsmen would pull it off. Total team effort. Victory was ours.

We started batting, and the runs racked up. This was going to be sweet: The Australian team and its fans looked dejected. All they could do was hope for a sporting miracle.

Well, we needed to make 43 more runs to win the game, and we had eight people left to bat—eight people! But then, it all fell apart. We lost those final eight wickets and made only 37 runs, losing by five runs.

There was silence all across the Caribbean. Disbelief! This did not just happen to us.

Two days later, the numbness was still there. We could not even speak about it. Many of us at the Calypso Spectacular hoped the carnival-like atmosphere would help us to move on. Once we got to the stadium, heard the music, and saw the crowd of partygoers, it did. The dancing began with reckless abandon, and all was right in our world once again.

But then David Rudder came to the stage.

David Rudder has been one of the preeminent calypsonians for decades. In 1996 he could do no wrong as a performer. One of his most popular songs was "Rally Round the West Indies," a song calling on the Caribbean people not to give up on the West Indies cricket team. It spoke of the glory days of the team and assured us that it would come again with all of our support.

Well, on March 16, 1996, we did not want to support the team. All was lost. There was no way we thought David would sing that song.

But the man would not be deterred. His band struck up the all too familiar tune we had been humming for years, and he walked onto the stage.

We booed. We did not want to hear it, and we booed the great David Rudder. He looked at us, understanding, and said something to the effect of "I know you are upset. I feel your pain too. But it is now, more than ever, that we need to sing this song."

He sang—no, more than that—he educated us on our team, its greatness, and what it meant to us as a people. He continued in his melodious voice and willed us to understand why we needed to sing this song together.

And join him we did, thousands strong, as far as the eyes could see. We joined in and sang, "Rally! Rally round the West Indies. Now and forever!"[2]

---

2 Rudder, David, "Rally Round the West Indies," *The Gilded Collection 1986–89*, released in 1993.

Cricket

I have reflected on that moment many times over the years, particularly as I traveled the world and met people who remembered the glory days of the West Indies cricket team.

In Australia, I was offered free beer all night because I was a distant relative of one of the former captains. On Air New Zealand, I was a celebrity with the crew because I was from the West Indies, home of the greats. Many times, speaking to people from India, Pakistan, or Sri Lanka, I listened to their stories about my team's triumphs over theirs during that period. They are, of course, happy that this is no longer the case.

One of my favorite stories of the team was told by a gentleman from Papua New Guinea. I was seeking his support for an important issue. When we met, I started my pitch as to why he should support the cause, but he stopped me in midsentence and said, "You already have my support. I did not come here to speak about that issue. I came to discuss cricket with you."

At the time, I was caught off guard. I thanked him for his support and asked how much he knew of the team. He laughed and intimated that as a child he had admired these islanders who would come to Australia, New Zealand, and England to win over and over again. These victories gave him hope, as an islander, that his dreams too were possible, that he could accomplish them.

I always smile when I reflect on this and understand why the sentiment is to "Rally Round the West Indies." I hope the players understand what their victories mean, not only to their fans in the Caribbean but all over the world. Sometimes, it is not just a game.

Sometimes, it means a whole lot more to people who are looking on, who are inspired by what you represent, and whom you may not even be aware of.

The Caribbean Outdoors

In the Caribbean, we love being outside. This is a major part of our socialization process. Some of our happiest moments are at street parties or beach parties. In St. Kitts, the strip makes the perfect Friday night. It is a row of beach huts, each with a different appeal, whether food, music, or entertainment. Standing there at night with the ocean breeze hitting your face while enjoying the latest music and the drink of your choice is the ideal island escape.

In Barbados, the Oistins Fish Fry has taken that scene to another level with a section for older persons to enjoy "back-in-time" music to which they ballroom dance. There's a little something for everyone.

This outdoors Friday night scene occurs across the entire Caribbean. In St. Lucia, a song was created especially for the Gros Islet Friday night session.

Early in our lives, we Caribbean islanders spend recess outside, playing in a field, or at our school fairs or church bazaars, held outside as well. We play all of our sports outside without the benefit of covering, and if it rains, we continue until our mothers scream warnings at us to get inside before we "catch cold."

During the carnival, our dancing is mainly in the streets or in outdoor stadiums. When I studied in Trinidad, I experienced my first "Trini" carnival in 1999, and whether it was a social on the docks overlooking the water where we danced to groovy soca or "jamming" through the streets of Port of Spain and around the Savannah, it was definitely an unbelievable experience.

I remember taking a break and sitting next to a cul-de-sac while the band moved on because we were just too tired after partying through the night for a third straight night. My friends grabbed some corn soup, and we figured we would catch up to the action once we got our second wind.

But as the party moved up the street, another one kicked in for all of the stragglers resting around us. One DJ with the latest carnival tunes and an enthusiastic crowd indicated there would be no rest until midnight. The party had to continue.

But perhaps my best carnival memory of that year was Machel Montano's introduction to his set at the Boy Scouts Fete.

Now Machel Montano is one of the best carnival performers of his generation. He started as a preteen singing "Too Young to Soca" and has been entertaining us ever since. I've seen him perform in St. Kitts, Barbados, Trinidad, Guyana, and New York. I missed him in Canada and Notting Hill, but there's always next year. He has never disappointed. He was once scheduled to perform at Madison Square Garden on the same night as a teen pop star. He was given the smaller room, which was sold out shortly after the tickets went on sale. Many West Indians in New York who did not get tickets were disappointed, but Machel agreed to perform another show that night in the same venue. Two shows in one night is pretty impressive, considering the frenetic pace of soca performers. I was among those who got tickets to the second show. When it was all finally over and we had left the Garden, one of the staff members, in complete bewilderment, asked the crowd outside, "Who is this guy? He sold out twice in one night at the Garden."

The crowd's response? "That's Machel, people. MACHEL!"

During my first Trinidad carnival, his introductory song was "Powder Puff." The lights throughout the stadium went out, and all we had were the stars. Then, the early beats of the song kicked in, and the crowd got excited. One light streamed through the crowd, and there they were, the Powder Posse, moving toward the stage. The crowd of thousands cleared the way for them as they "chipped" onward, throwing powder into the night sky.

The music ramped up, and the lights grew. Behind the Powder Posse, a truck crawled through with Machel on top, singing,

Puff! Ah wey me powder posse,
Puff! Lemme see the gloves in the air.
Puff! Ah wey me powder posse,
Sprinkle it like you just don't care.[3]

The crowd burst with excitement with each crescendo and a dance session for the ages. I remained in the middle of it all with the powder floating onto my face, feeling just as alive as everyone else there.

When Machel got to the stage, the party continued, but the introduction and the build-up were simply amazing. He has replicated this many times over the years, with different songs, but there truly is nothing like the first time.

Being a witness to this made me reflect on the significance of carnival in general and our calypsonians in particular.

Caribbean carnivals and calypso music represent elements of Caribbean culture that have helped to define us as a people. Whether

---

3 "Powder Puff," Machel Montano and Xtatic, *Any Minute Now*, released in 1999.

it is a part of that symbolic conclusion to the annual sugar cane harvest of old or a part of the commemoration of the anniversary of our emancipation from slavery or a part of the Christmas celebration or a part of the pre-Lent activities, carnival represents Caribbean history. Each island tells a different and fascinating tale of the origin and significance of the carnival, which, while being unique to that specific island, is also part of the Caribbean reality in general.

Calypso, as a complement to the carnival, helps us to make social commentary in song because the music, even the fast-paced, party tunes, tends to make some reference to an occurrence or person of interest during the year.

Both are integral to our oral and visual history. Our calypsonians and carnival band leaders have become icons because of their creativity in telling that Caribbean story and showcasing the beauty of our culture.

They are a fundamental part of the Caribbean way of life, which everyone is encouraged to experience at least once.

The Caribbean's Place in the World

There have also been many instances when unsung Caribbean people have helped to generate change in the wider international community.

I was not aware of how much people from around the world looked to us until I traveled outside. But the interactions I've had the privilege of experiencing have made me even prouder of my fellow West Indians.

I once met this amazing gentleman from South Africa. He was a giant of a man within the global community, campaigning for the advancement of people from the developing world. I was in awe just to have a conversation with him, and I developed goose bumps as we talked.

"Hello, young fellow. How are you?" he asked.
I replied, "I am doing well, sir, and how are you?"
"Just fine. Just fine. And how are things in Sandy Point?"

I paused in shock. You have to know St. Kitts to ask about Sandy Point. What did this champion of the underclass, this figure in the international community, know about Sandy Point? He laughed as he saw my quizzical look. He said, "You did not know I had visited your island did you? I was there in the 1980s when I was still in exile. I could not return to South Africa then, but my Caribbean brothers and sisters took me in. I met with several influential people in your country and the Caribbean who spoke with me about the antiapartheid struggle. They all wanted to help and had been speaking against it for many years. It was a refuge for me back then."

I came of age in the 1980s when Nelson Mandela was still imprisoned and apartheid was still a scourge on human society. The antiapartheid movement had, by then, become a global cause.

Until that moment, I was unaware of the Caribbean role in the movement. I started to research this and saw that many Caribbean leaders had been publicly denouncing the ideology everywhere they went for many years. They had been strong advocates and supported the cause in whatever way they could from the other side of the world. I was told, on another occasion, during my research of the Caribbean and the antiapartheid movement, that it was the Caribbean countries that first instituted a cricketing ban on South Africa in the 1970s because of its policy of apartheid. This ban spread throughout the cricketing world and remained until apartheid was no more. When I came of age in the 1980s, I knew of the ban and why it existed, but I knew nothing of our role in originating it.

It made me proud to be Caribbean. We understood injustice, and we were not afraid to stand on principle.

It was gratifying to know our efforts had not been in vain, and seeing this man taking the global stage, still appreciative of my country's goodwill to him, was special to me.

Chapter 2

GLOBAL ARCHIPELAGO: EXAMINING THE ISLAND WAY OF LIFE AROUND THE WORLD

View from Brimstone Hill, St. Kitts. (Photo courtesy of Sally Richardson.)

What of the other islands out there? I had to know more about the other islanders. This island trek was not only about these other lands. It was also about learning more of myself, an islander who had previously held the extreme beliefs mentioned earlier and now had a love of islands and a quest for understanding more about their place in the world. This island journey would simultaneously help my exploration of the islander's psyche.

In 2013 I had the opportunity to explore these and many more thoughts about the islands. Being an islander, I wanted to understand if there were any significant commonalities among islanders, not just those from the Caribbean but also from islands the world over. I was fortunate to be working at the UN on island issues when preparations for the Third International Conference on Small Island Developing States were taking place, so I could travel to these islands and have many of my questions answered.

I had an understanding of islands long before that, but I don't think I developed a full appreciation until I visited three islands in three different parts of the world, over the course of three weeks. This deepened my love of islands.

Until that time, I was of the view that all of these islands were very different in their cultures and histories. It used to annoy me that many non-islanders would group all islands into one homogenous collection under the banner of "islands," without appreciating their diversity.

They are, however, diverse. Even within regions, each individual island has its own unique identity, which is different from all else. But we islanders also can identify with each other because we are islanders. We do have much in common, despite our differences, as I would learn from my trips.

Impressions from Trips in 2013

JAMAICA

Billboard in Kingston, Jamaica.

Jamaica is one of the better-known Caribbean islands, and there are several reasons why this is so. Whether because of its tourist hotspots; the cultural icons, including Bob Marley; or the reigning fastest person in the world, Usain Bolt, somehow or other, Jamaica remains nestled in our global social consciousness when thinking of island culture.

Jamaicans who have been weaned on the greatness of their heroes have a sense of accomplishment and pride. Jamaicans are confident.

They have made their mark on the world many times and will continue to do so.

Once I arrived in Jamaica, I felt an instant familiarity. The vibe was so similar to what I knew, coming from another Caribbean island. And as far as anyone could tell, I could very well be Jamaican. I was so acquainted with the pulse of the island that, in a heartbeat, I fell into step to the caress of the land. It simply felt like home.

Throughout Kingston and the other locations I visited, the cultural and historical presence loomed great in the stores and architecture. I could see the colonial past, the postcolonial prominence, the African heritage, and the promise of the future. I saw how this small island could produce so many artists and other great figures. The place just oozes creativity and energy. Beyond the cities and the famous beaches, the wide open spaces of the countryside are worth seeing, especially with the mountain ranges always in view.

Love of Sports and Food

Sunday afternoon in the Caribbean is very sports-centric: if you're not actually attending a sporting event, you're watching it on television.

It was easy for me to assimilate the Jamaican custom by spending my Sunday afternoon at the Kingston restaurant of the one and only Usain Bolt, the world's fastest man. Where else would one best merge food and sport in Jamaica?

So at Tracks and Records I had an amazing sampling of red pea soup, codfish fritters, jerk chicken, and festival, which Jamaicans call cornbread fritters, all washed down with a local ginger beer. Just thinking about it makes my mouth water once again. Each dish can be filling and quite satisfying on its own, but not being in the

Caribbean for a while, having been living in North America at the time, I needed to be reminded of all that was pleasing.

The restaurant was a beehive of activity. Not only was it a popular destination, but on this day, there were two sporting events pulling the crowds.

One was on television. The West Indies cricket team was caught in a thrilling limited overs match, a cricket competition that takes place during the course of an entire day. This particular match was against the reigning world champion, India.

The actual game was taking place a few miles away at Sabina Park to a packed crowd, but I arrived in Kingston too late to attend it. So on to Tracks and Records I ventured and loved watching every minute of the game on television.

In cricket there are times when the outcome has been determined long in advance and the game can stretch on for days. However, for those with a shorter attention span and the more adrenaline junky types, the "limited overs" version is your game. In this format, a set amount of balls are bowled, and the batting team must try to make as many runs as possible. Afterward, it switches with the other team, which must bat the same number of balls to get more runs.

This was the type of game I saw when I walked into Tracks and Records. The West Indies team had fielded first and were now at bat, trailing India. As the hour rolled on, it looked as though they would have an easy victory. They soon had just 27 runs to make off 72 balls. Easy, right? Not so in cricket; one or two lost wickets and the entire complexion of the game changes.

So I stopped to enjoy my red pea soup, reminiscing on a time when this was a Saturday afternoon delight for me back home in St. Kitts. I reopened my eyes and, wouldn't you know it, another wicket was lost, and we had to find a way to score 18 runs off 54 balls with only the closing batsmen remaining.

Now I was fixated on the screen, as was everyone else in the room. Ball after ball, run after run, we tightened up, unsure of how this would end, electricity filling the air.

Finally, the bowler bowled, the batsman hit, and we made the final two runs needed. The Windies (as we call the team) won by one wicket with only 14 balls remaining.

Pandemonium in the restaurant: Nobody celebrates as Jamaicans do.

Kingston, Jamaica. (Photo courtesy of Sheree Chambers.)

In Jamaica I was always impressed with the beauty of the land. I remember that while on vacation there a few years earlier, driving from Kingston to Port Antonio, the landscape and views removed any sense of time in me as I was taken in by their splendor.

There is much agricultural activity throughout the mountain range, and driving along the coast allows your imagination about the history of this island to run wild.

When I drove across Jamaica, I could not help but remember a video I once saw. Someone had filmed a drive around Jamaica after Hurricane Gilbert in 1988 and given the video the soundtrack of Jimmy Cliff's "Many Rivers to Cross." Years later, when YouTube was invented, the video was posted, making it possible for the world to see. Here I was, driving along the same route, witnessing the resilience of the Jamaican people. They took Hurricane Gilbert on the chin but did not stay down.

I also thought about Ian Fleming moving to Jamaica and having this same coastline view when he wrote his James Bond tales. And, of course, I thought of Bob Marley and the inspiration he took from this land and its people, melding it into his songs.

I had heard about Boston Beach where the best jerk chicken could be found, so I was brimming with excitement in anticipation of sampling this delicacy in the land considered its birthplace.

When we arrived, we could not find any jerk chicken vendors. We thought that strange but soon realized why. The National Men's Relay Team was about to race somewhere in the world, and nothing else mattered until it finished. We joined in, of course. This is always a must-see event. Usain Bolt was not merely Jamaican to me; he was Caribbean and deserved my support.

The race was not close. I forget who was runner up, but the national pride remained intact; the Jamaican national team was victorious.

The jerk chicken lived up to the hype. It was mouthwatering, though I did have to drink water repeatedly to sooth the burning in my mouth. Jerk is definitely not for the weak.

This and every time I leave Jamaica, I feel inspired by the many wonderful stories and the many great people with whom I share a common island bond.

FIJI

A bure in Nadi, Fiji.

My trip from Jamaica to Fiji was very long, flying from Jamaica to Miami, Los Angeles, New Zealand, and finally Fiji, totaling almost 30 hours. All of this meant that when I arrived early in the morning, I was probably not at my most sociable.

However, as I walked into the terminal, an airport worker looked at me, smiled, and said, "Bula, brother, bula."

Now, the word *bula* has several different meanings in the Caribbean, not all of them quite friendly, but fortunately, I had been alerted to what *bula* meant in Fiji.

I did not know what to reply, though, so I nodded and went my way. Later, the man saw me and in a rather surprised manner asked, "You're not Fijian? Where are you from?"

The minute he learned that I was from the Caribbean, he was excited.

"The islands from the other side," this man gleefully exclaimed, "far from home, but here, you are family."

How can anyone stay unsociable with a greeting like that? I engaged him, and we exchanged tales of our respective islands and regions. I was the first person from the Caribbean he had ever met, and he wanted to know all there was to know. His curiosity reminded me of my own fascination with meeting people from different places around the world. I related very well to his queries.

Fiji is full of places to visit and tour. I stayed in Nadi and took a tour of five must-see sites: a Hindu temple, the local market, an arts and craft store, the Garden of the Sleeping Giant, and the natural hot springs. What I learned about these places was that even though tourists visit them, they are also places that the local population frequent regularly. They are part of the everyday life of Fiji, so here I was, being both tourist and local.

You cannot spend time in Fiji without visiting these places. Through them, you instantly learn so much about the island and its people. Fiji is a multicultural, multiethnic, and multidenominational country. I saw churches, mosques, and temples as I traveled around.

Village chiefs play an important role in the cultural, political, economic, and social life of the island. They are revered and treated with a high level of respect. When my tour group saw one of the chiefs, who was in council with the village elders, we observed that everyone close by was silent as the chief and elders walked past. Our guide requested that we also remain silent around the chief, and, very naturally, we obeyed. We felt a sense of reverence around him.

The Garden of the Sleeping Giant was a beautiful nature reserve, just up Queens Road to the north of Nadi. If you look at the mountain range from just the right angle, you can behold the sleeping giant who bestows his name. It is this natural beauty that is one of the many delights of islands the world over. Such sites might not be well known when compared to other more famous natural sites around the world, whether America's Grand Canyon or Australia's Uluru, but they still impart that same sense of wonder and awe. I felt so at peace on this journey through Nadi, and I know that the environment around me contributed to that.

Garden of the Sleeping Giant, Fiji.

But the man-made wonders also grabbed me. I was very much intrigued by the marketplace in Nadi. In the Caribbean, the market is integral to our culture and history, a place where all the local farmers, fishermen, and butchers once came to sell their produce.

Beyond its necessary commercial function, the market was also a social hot spot of news gathering, political campaigning, and everyday interactions.

I remember going to the market on Saturday mornings with my parents. It was an overwhelming experience for a child, with its fast-paced, loud, aggressive activity, but it was also exciting. It allowed us to connect fully with an early form of local economic activity for pre-independence and, later, postcolonial societies, before international economic endeavors burst forth, linking us to the world through globalization.

In recent years in St. Kitts, that type of marketplace activity is no more. The market is still there, and there is some activity, but the marketplace's role as the central focus of social and economic interaction is gone.

In Nadi, seeing this bustling marketplace brought back some of my wonderful childhood memories. I should say that there were many supermarkets in Fiji, but the alternative of the market was there also and was doing quite well.

I walked around, fascinated that, on the other side of the world, an island with no connection to mine, without the past that we have experienced, had a similar construct. The fruits and vegetables may have had different names, but they were the same or very similar to what I knew. Even buying a coconut to drink the water and eat the jelly inside offered the same experience as it did at home, especially when the lady at the stand cut off a piece of the coconut shell for me to use as a spoon.

My visit made me a fan of Fiji. When I arrived there, I felt, for the first time in my travels around the world, that I was far from home. However, the friendly nature of the Fijians made me feel right at home with them. When I visited the arts and craft shop, every Fijian smiled at me and gave me the usual "Bula." *Bula* means "Hello," and yet, so much more than "Hello." I interpret it as "Welcome to us." By then, I knew that I simply had to reply with my own, "Bula," and a smile as well.

Then, they would engage me in conversation. There was no sense of intrusion on my part; I was most comfortable because this island and its people felt so open and welcoming, and everything seemed so similar. The buildings were the same; the children walking home from school brought flashbacks of my days doing the same; the strong sports culture and the sense of community all felt like home. It is indeed true that many of these traits and activities exist in other countries. These things are not exclusive to the islands, but for me, the vibe felt the same. It's that island connection that I did not think existed. Yet I found it does.

That is what it was. And while reminding me about my own heritage and culture, Fiji brought me home to the islands again.

Another word I learned in Fiji is *vinaka*, meaning "Thank you."

Bula, Fiji. *Vinaka.*

When I was in Fiji, I visited the Mamanuca archipelago and stayed on Malolo Island for a few days. To get there, I left Nadi from Denarau Harbor and sailed for two hours along the archipelago. On the boat, there was the nicest Fijian lady who told us to call her Ma. She was our concierge, and she reminded me of the tough but care-taking, nurturing women I knew back home in St. Kitts.

Ma was always smiling and checking to see if we were okay. She would slide out of our cabin on a routine sweep of the boat, and during one of those sweeps, a gentleman slipped into our cabin and took up one of the spare seats. The rest of us were indifferent to this, not realizing that each cabin had its own passenger list and that the tickets looked different. I was not sure if there was a variation in the costs or class of tickets and, perhaps, this gentleman assumed that one cabin was as good as the other. He lay down and went to sleep on the couch.

Ma returned with her cheery, wide smile and asked, "Does anyone need anything? Remember to ask Ma if you do."

She looked around and, suddenly, stopped smiling and zeroed in on the intruder, snoring away. She moved quickly across the cabin, very serious, and nudged him gently.

"Sir," she whispered. "Ticket please."

The gentleman woke up and did not have the appropriate ticket. Ma would not tolerate this. He was disrupting her calm order of passengers behaving nicely.

"No ticket, you go!" She instructed firmly and marched him out of the cabin. She then turned around to us, and the smile had returned, oblivious, almost, to the interruption.

"Do you need juice, chips, tea? No? Okay, when you do, just call Ma. I'll look after you."

Almost by instinct everyone in the cabin nodded, avoiding eye contact. We did not want to upset Ma.

Likuliku Lagoon Resort, Fiji.

Likuliku Lagoon Resort stands near the ocean like a dream. It is beautifully built with bures, the straw roofed mini-huts indigenous to the region, on the beach or on stilts over the water. I selected an overwater bure and found that so much of my time was spent admiring the colorful fish swimming around under the glass floor fitted into the room. It was soothing.

I found the extremes of the tide in Fiji dramatic. In St. Kitts we never see such a contrast between low tide and high tide, but in Fiji the tides rise and fall by several meters. That's when you see just how close to shore the coral reef clings and how delicate it is.

Twice a day, a seaplane would land a slight distance from my bure. I would time my activities around the arrival of the plane. I had never before seen one land so close.

One day, a storm raged through the region, and a little cabin fever set in. So, when it passed, I felt the need to break the monotony of being indoors. I had heard of a village tour on the other side of the island and thought it would be nice to learn more about the native customs.

I set out to the pier and saw possibly the smallest boat ever made. I looked around for the larger one to take us to the village, but this was it. This meant that if there were waves to be felt, we would feel them. And feel them we did. Even though the storm had moved on from the island, it was still somewhere in the region. The waves were an indication of this: they were rough.

Now, I'm an islander, and it is normally expected that we islanders have some confidence with respect to knowledge of the seas. Indeed, it is that knowledge that makes us humble. We know what the ocean can do.

So after the first hit of the waves against this motor-driven dinghy, I had an "oh oh, this was not a good idea" moment. After the tenth hit, with the boat being the plaything of the ocean, I was terrified. We had no life vests, I could not see the shore, as my back was to it, and the captain was a madman, shrieking with glee at the excitement, every time the waves slammed into the front of the boat, making us fly.

"We are doomed," I thought. Would this boat ever dock? We must have been traveling close to an hour.

"Whee!" the captain bellowed, while I glared at him. I didn't care anymore. I was sitting on the floor. Sitting on the makeshift seats next to the ledge of the boat, while only using our hands to hold on, was not very comforting. I was convinced we would fall over into the great beyond at any second. This must have been how they felt in the third movie of the series *Pirates of the Caribbean*, when they were trying to find Captain Jack Sparrow, heading to the edges of the earth.[4]

---

4 "At World's End" from *Pirates of the Caribbean* movie series, directed by Gore Verbinski, produced by Jerry Bruckheimer, Walt Disney Pictures, 2007.

I looked over at the Fijian lady sitting calmly on the edge of the boat with her sunglasses on. She must have made this trip countless times, but all I was thinking was, "Do you not fear death?"

Finally, we turned away from the waves and headed toward land. It did not seem too far away now. I was never so happy to see the familiar sight of coconut trees.

We got to the village and walked around, learning of the local customs and the history of this particular community. Apparently, at some time in the past, the old chief had passed on and his eldest son had become chief, as was the custom. However, the second son did not want to live under the reign of his brother and left with his supporters to form their own village where he would be the ruler. This was the village where I was standing on that day, that of the second son who had refused to obey the laws of the land but who, as chief, had now become the preserver of those same laws.

Ironically, this was a much smaller and less developed village than the first. It was at that point that I remembered my Shakespeare.

Thou, nature, art my goddess; to thy law
My services are bound. Wherefore should I
Stand in the plague of custom, and permit
The curiosity of nations to deprive me.[5]

This was the opening monologue of Edmund in *King Lear*, the beginning of act 1, scene 2, where the illegitimate son felt he too was entitled to the lands of the legitimate first born.

Curious that Shakespeare is applicable everywhere, once you know where to look. My literature teacher from high school would

---

5 Shakespeare, William, *King Lear*, act 1, scene 2, 1608.

be pleased that I still remember these lines. On a good note, in Fiji, rather than pursuing a Shakespearian tragedy of vengeance, despair, and loss, you just pack up with your supporters and find your own lands, a much more palatable solution on an island.

Following the tour, it was time for the kava ceremony. I did not know that this was part of the deal. I assumed we would just be observing and not be the main focus. But apparently, in Fiji, when you are invited to partake of kava with the villagers, they are welcoming you to them. You are now a part of the Fijian family.

The entire village sat around us and clapped as the village elder received our gift of powder to mix into the water, which together made the kava we were to drink. She mixed this in the specially made kava bowls and drank.

I was a bit hesitant, I confess, but I did not want to offend. I drank from the kava bowl, not quite sure what it would taste like. I had never tasted anything like it before. I smiled as I swallowed, so that they would be pleased. Then I clapped and shouted, "Bula!" Now I am Fijian.

I knew that the kava, a calming drink made from the root of the yaqona plant, would make my mouth numb, but it was not too intense a sensation. I was more focused on the church in the village. Inside, I prayed the boat ride back to Likuliku Lagoon Resort would be safe and fast.

The waves would surely be more favorable to us going in the other direction. Also, the sky had cleared, so I was hopeful.

My prayers were answered. As we started off, I was happy that this time around, I was facing inland. The waves were much calmer, so I breathed more easily. From my vantage point, the coastline was right there. I was now truly embarrassed; we were a few meters from the shore. With my back to the land, earlier, I had not been able to see this. Also, the ride back took less than ten minutes. This could not have been the same route. But it was! We sailed past the same buoys. My impression that we had traveled for close to an hour was the result of my terrified mind playing tricks on me.

We were never in any real danger. That was why the captain was enjoying the ride and the older lady in the sunglasses was so nonchalant.

As I reflected on it, I remembered my childhood at Newtown Primary School. Walking home from school, I passed many fishing boats that were the same size as this one in Fiji. In fact, the boats were identical, as I think about it more.

This was how it was. No matter whether the waves were rough but manageable or the sea was calm—especially if it was calm—the fishermen ventured out to fish. My young eyes found it fascinating. I wanted to go out with them, as many young people living close to the ocean do. Years later, here I was on the other side of the world doing just that and being fearful.

I wondered if we had, as islanders, lost the basics of being islanders, or was it just me? Had I been living away from the islands for too long? How many other islanders no longer have their island instincts because they have focused on the outside world more? Was I the only one, or is it common? In my Fiji journey I felt a desire to reconnect to the islands even more than I previously had.

After getting the Caribbean perspective on island issues in Jamaica, followed by the Pacific view in Fiji, the third and final part of this island trek, taken to prepare for the 2014 conference, was a visit to the Seychelles to get the perspective of the African, Indian Ocean, and South China Sea islands.

THE SEYCHELLES

Hotel in Mahé, Seychelles.

I left Fiji early in the morning and set out for the Seychelles. I traveled through Australia and the United Arab Emirates to get to this island nation in the Indian Ocean. The trip lasted 27 hours and again took its toll, but when I arrived, I witnessed one of the most beautiful places I had ever seen.

NATURE REVISITED

The islanders refer to the country as the Garden of Eden, and it is easy to see why. There is unspoiled beauty everywhere.

One of the first things I observed was the ever-present feel of the mountains and the ocean. They were everywhere at once. While driving, you could be right on the edge of the water, make one turn, and be in the mountains. They were that close to each other.

While in the Seychelles, I learned that these islands did not have an original, indigenous population. So everything was, in a way, imported, new, a mix uniquely created by those who went there. There was evidence of both English and French influence, and when the people spoke, the singsong accent of St. Lucians from the Caribbean filled my ears. St. Lucia also has a strong English and French past, and when I arrived in the Seychelles, it was as though the islands had once been one, single island that had, somehow, separated.

I learned as I spent time there that people from the Seychelles are very much in tune with the Caribbean. I could hear the music from Jamaican artists on both the radio and television, while I enjoyed the Creole sounds of *zouk* and cadence wherever I walked.

The islanders in the Seychelles have a love of their home. They understand that preservation of the environment is of paramount importance and try to live a life of protecting the natural habitat. The many hotels were built to blend into the landscape so that the unspoiled beauty remained. This impressed me wherever I went and was evident beyond merely the physical. You could feel it in the music, dance, art, and songs of the people. They all brought with them an awareness of the need for preservation.

The Seychelles were the chosen honeymoon destination of Prince William and Kate, and many young couples from Europe and the Persian Gulf have walked around, enjoying these nature-filled islands. I could see why. The Seychelles make you relax. The restaurants have an easygoing feel whether they are in the mountains or on the beach. Everywhere I ventured, I heard my island music accompanying me, and, again, I felt at home.

The island of Mahé in the Seychelles has a marketplace, similar to the one I had seen in Fiji and the one from my childhood. The parallels were everywhere.

A NIGHT ON THE TOWN

Mahé is extremely mountainous. On a few occasions, depending on the speed of the vehicle you are traveling in around these mountains, your stomach may feel the trip as much as you do. But it is all so picturesque and exciting, you forget this quickly.

I remember going to dinner one night on the other side of the island, and just getting there was an adventure in itself. The bus hurtled down the narrow mountain roads, twisting and turning as it veered along the path. I felt nauseous from the bobbing and weaving but refrained from complaining, and no one else did either.

There were no lights on the road, so the darkness had a staccato flow of illumination as we drove past the occasional house poking out from among the foliage or the full moon peeking through the swaying branches of the 100-year-old trees.

I held the door handle for comfort, though, in reality, what security could there be when there were no barriers separating the road from the steep slope of the land?

Funnily enough, I had had a similar experience while gripping a car door handle during a drive through the mountains of St. Lucia, many years earlier. Mahé and St. Lucia were like twin islands.

"Is this really worth it?" I wondered as the driver whistled quietly while listening to local music that had that ever-so-recognizable island sound. Perhaps, I could suggest that he slow down. Would I be considered "soft" among the group? Everyone else was laughing and regaling each other with tales of the day. I, however, was riding "shotgun," so they could not feel what I did. Surely, they didn't understand.

Before I could conjure up the courage to ask him to slow down, the driver made one sharp left turn, and we found ourselves driving along the coast. "Impossible," I thought. "We were just at the top of the island looking down."

A few moments later, we were in the main area of the city with shops, banks, and people milling around us. The architecture was rustic and beautiful.

We pulled over to a restaurant on the beach, and the aroma hit me. "Oh, this smells so good!" I exclaimed, forgetting my earlier digestive woes. This was going to be fun.

Two hours later, I had consumed some of the best food known to man and topped it off with a cool drink of coconut water, picked from the trees in the back. The easy-listening, romantic reggae in the background soothed my sensibilities even more, while the lapping waves nearby made this a most perfect evening.

To answer my earlier question: yes, this was definitely worth it. This island had it all: adventure and excitement, cool vibes, great food, wonderful music, beautiful people, and pristine views.

The drive back to the hotel was one filled with quiet reflection on the night out. If there were any problems with the drive, I wouldn't have known. I was now fully in island mode.

APHRODISIAC

The Seychelles has a nut called coco der mer, a double-sided coconut that resembles a pair of brown, striped lungs, or to some eyes, a voluptuous backside. It is almost held sacred by the people there.

I was told by a craft shop owner that these trees were protected by the government and that I would not be able to take away any of the fruit. Apparently, it is an aphrodisiac, according to the locals, which pretty much explains why any government would have to protect it from honeymooners or anyone else for that matter.

The dynamics of the coco der mer were also quite amusing. There is a male tree and a female tree. It was incredibly easy to decipher which was which. I, unfortunately, only saw this dynamo in pictures. The trees were only found on the island of Praslin, and I did not have an opportunity to travel there. But this only means that I will have to return to seek out this elusive aphrodisiac for myself.

The Seychelles are a five-hour flight from either the United Arab Emirates or South Africa. This Indian Ocean island nation was colonized by both the English and the French. Their colonial descendants live throughout the country, and from my vantage point during that visit, there was peaceful coexistence. This was important to me, as a fellow islander from a region with similar cultural dynamics.

However, there was something I could not overtly observe that made me slightly uncomfortable while there.

MEMORIES OF A PAINFUL PAST

I guess the origins of the strange feelings I experienced in the Seychelles came, in part, from my childhood.

Shortly after independence in 1983, St. Kitts and Nevis pursued tourism as an economic activity to counter the declining sugar industry. These were times when I marveled at the sailing hotels—as my younger self referred to them at the time—coming to our shores, as well as the flights filled with tourists. I loved visiting the hotels with their grandeur. However, at that time, I could only observe. This was not a part of my world. There was a slight feeling of rejection back then.

As I got older and my contemporaries sought employment, some of them worked in the tourist sector, but again, for them, the product was not to be enjoyed. It was a means of employment only.

When I began taking vacations, I stayed with family and friends, though I must acknowledge I knew some who did, in fact, vacation at hotels and resorts on neighboring islands. They were the privileged few.

And so, in the Seychelles, where many of the islanders work in the hotels, I suddenly remembered my own years of looking in from the outside, feeling that sting of denial, wondering and wishing I could experience such a life, if only for a moment. These reflections haunted me ever so briefly. I left the Seychelles with a renewed appreciation of the beauty of the islands but also reminded of that sense of dejection from my childhood.

The reality is that, for many islanders, the image of an exotic paradise does not ring true. The exotic paradise is their home, and it is filled with many challenges. Too often, islanders only see this "paradise" from the outside while living close to, and even working at, the amazing resorts.

Victoria, Seychelles.

The Seychelles, though, have a unique character, something I loved particularly. They were previously uninhabited islands, and I have never understood why. I wondered if what looked like rip currents about a mile from the coast had made them difficult for early sailors to navigate. Whatever the reason, the Seychelles now flourish as multicultural islands.

I witnessed a hardworking but also fun people. They were proud of their accomplishments but refused to rest on their laurels. On one of the few occasions when I got a break from work, I walked around the capital city, Victoria, during the day and saw the churches, the stores, and the market, along with the restaurants on the beach. What I liked most was the fact that trees that were, probably, over 100 years old stood among the buildings, with the construction taking place around them, ensuring they remained preserved. This was part of the respect for the environment that was prevalent throughout the Seychelles.

In the Pacific Islands, the respect for the environment is evident because the people have an historical link to the land going back generations. In the Caribbean we hold onto land because, in the past, we had been denied access to it, and so now there is an appreciation for it. What was the reason in the Seychelles with their very different history?

In the islands, land is limited. We know this very early in our lives because all around us there is the mighty ocean. So we understand the importance of preserving what we have. The Seychelles have wind farms harnessing the renewable energy sources around them as part of the people's commitment to sustainable development. Here was also a country at the forefront of the global warming fears of a rising ocean. The environmental policies here are also a way of educating the greater powers about what needs to be done for sustainability throughout the world.

Sustainable development had happily become a national policy in the Seychelles because the people understood the need to preserve the limited land that they had. This was home, and they knew that its protection was of the utmost importance. This was something I strongly admired about the islanders of the Seychelles.

I regret not being able to spend more time there and exploring more, but I am inspired to return. I found the people too nice for me to stay away. I want to learn more about their history and the cultural identity now forged out of the amalgamation of many others. I want to visit Praslin, the island where most of the coco der mer grows, just to be amused by the many aphrodisiac hunters. It is also important for me to reconcile the feeling of dejection I experienced while there.

What was it that brought that old feeling to the fore when all around me people tried their hardest to make me comfortable? I owe them this.

My trips to these islands in 2013 opened my eyes. I was consumed with so many thoughts, but the overriding sentiment was about the impact the journey was having on me. So I wondered how much greater the impact would be if I were to delve deeper into the island way of life. I would get the chance the following year, when the Third International Conference on Small Island Developing States would be held. Though representing the UN at this juncture, my perspective remained that of an islander. There, surrounded by others like me from across the globe, I would begin to place within a broader context the nascent thoughts with which I was coming to terms.

It was at this conference that I would see the enormity of the issues affecting islands across the globe and possible solutions to them. It was also at the conference in Samoa that I was able to separate the issues and focus on the central point of the discussion: the island people.

Chapter 3

TRANSFORMATION IN SAMOA: THE CONFERENCE THAT CHANGED MY LIFE

Fire dancer in Samoa.

During the summer of 2014, I traveled to the Independent State of Samoa, a visit I had been looking forward to for several years. But this trip was not a vacation. It was the culmination of what I had been working on professionally for two years. The international community had come together to look at the challenges that small island developing states were facing and try to work out strategies to overcome these concerns.

Samoan Cultural Group.

My interest in the islands, from both an academic and professional perspective, now spanned more than 20 years.

SIDS had first gained international attention during the Earth Summit in 1992. It was felt, during this UN Conference on Environment and Development, that SIDS were special cases due to their vulnerabilities and required additional consideration.[6]

The small size of these islands; their distance and remoteness from major economic hubs; their ecological fragility; and their susceptibility to climate change, natural disasters, and fluctuations in the

6 Agenda 21: Programme of Action for Sustainable Development, 17.124, United Nations ISBN: 92-1-100509-4.

global economic environment were seen to produce major hurdles for sustainable development.[7]

One major outcome of the Earth Summit, for islands, was the call to convene a global conference to focus on the sustainable development of small island developing states. This meeting, which brought world leaders together to discuss the affairs of islands, was held in Barbados in 1994, when I was a student there at the University of the West Indies.

We could not escape the news of this conference in the papers and on the television even if we had wanted to. We also held discussions at the university about the significance of this conference, and it marked the first time, really, that I started getting a sense of what I would like to focus on, professionally.

This had quite an impact on me and helped to spur my fascination with the UN and island affairs. I joined the foreign service in part to work on this because I wanted to have a role in my island's voice in the international community.

In 2005, the ten-year review of that first island conference was held in Mauritius. Unfortunately, despite the gains that had been made in some islands over that ensuing decade, most still faced significant economic, environmental, and social challenges.

In Mauritius, I was one of the many island delegates, proud to be representing St. Kitts and Nevis and determined to take that step forward in the affairs of islands. It was quite an experience for me. It was as though a floodlight had been clicked on and things were so much clearer. I understood things I just would not have been able to grasp from the outside, as a student. I started, as well, to understand the way the UN operated and why, despite the best intentions, islands

7 Ibid.

were still in need of international support to succeed in their sustainable development strategies. There were many "moving parts" and processes that all needed to fit into place. There were many players in the international arena, all fighting to ensure that their specific needs were serviced, and in the midst of this, islands needed the means to implement the initiatives.

We felt that in Mauritius we had filled the necessary gaps and that this time it would be better. It would have been nice if we had not needed a third conference, but we did. SIDS were still struggling, and, in fact, the international community noted during the UN Conference on Sustainable Development in 2012 that, according to the findings of the review of the Mauritius Conference (MSI+5 review), many islands had regressed.[8]

The frequency of hurricanes and other natural disasters, the global economic and financial crisis, health challenges of both communicable and noncommunicable diseases, and climate change all affected the islands.

I wanted to do more this time, not just from the point of view of my island alone but with a comprehension of and focus on all islands. I wanted to further understand why we still faced challenges and how we could overcome them. I joined the UN in time to be a part of the organizing team of the conference, and it was here that my island appreciation reached its zenith. In Samoa, though I was one of the staff of the UN, I would be surrounded by others like me, others who were raised on the islands. Some stayed at home, leading their native lands to greatness. Others went out into the world, learning new methods, always with the islands of their birthplace foremost within their minds.

---

8 "The Future We Want," paragraph 178, United Nations, 12-53641-October 2012-500.

My responsibilities at the conference were extensive, allowing me to have an overview of all that was taking place. As part of the team, my responsibilities included monitoring and facilitating the negotiations of the outcome document, planning side events, and summarizing the statements of world leaders. I also recorded discussions in which the private sector engaged the islands, seeking ways to stimulate economic activities and promote enterprise in the islands, and I observed the civil society organizations ensuring that the affairs of all members of island societies were addressed.

All islands represented there expressed their concerns and their hopes for a better future for themselves and their children. Seeing it all from this perspective and connecting each individual dot, I was able to envision an island picture with its people at its core. This was where it began and ended: with the people.

One of the issues that resonated most with me was what we referred to as means of implementation. Financing, access to technology and innovation, capacity building, and partnerships were all important elements that would ensure that the decisions and blueprint for sustainable development of the islands could occur. It was an insufficiency of the means of implementation, in the past, that had limited the progress of the previous two meetings. This was where I now wanted to focus.

Strengthening the resilience of islanders and helping to educate all islanders, including those in the most remote islands, were fundamental, as was working on ways to ensure that these islanders were safe from storms and rising seas and that they were healthy and able to provide for themselves and their families despite the many external economic fluctuations and environmental scares.

Two particular events that I helped to organize dealt with strengthening resilience and with addressing debt sustainability.

From the Earth Summit in 1992, the global community understood that the major challenge for islanders was their vulnerability to economic and environmental shocks. It was this vulnerability that would set the islands back, over the years, whenever they sought developmental initiatives. In Grenada, for example, Hurricane Ivan, in 2004, destroyed most of the infrastructure and economic sectors on the island. So helping to organize this discussion among island leaders and international organizations was important to me, as I needed to hear the stories from other islanders but also try to conceptualize solutions to these vulnerabilities.

The other event, dealing with debt sustainability, was equally important. It looked at island challenges from another angle. In some respects, for many islands, debt grew as a result of trying to recover from the natural disasters and reconstruction. There were other factors related to the high debt, such as loan repayments, but the point was that trying to overcome the debt made island governments face hard choices in their sustainable development. What do you pay less attention to when so much is important? Not an ideal choice.

But at the core of these and many other discussions was how the people were affected. If a hurricane struck and the buildings were destroyed, it was the people who needed shelter; if the economic sectors were affected, it was the people who needed decent jobs; and if a government had to choose between paying off a loan and building a school, it was the island children who would be affected if their needs were not met.

In Samoa, these thoughts were no longer abstractions, because I was there, physically, with the island people who mattered for me. I felt very strongly that all of us islanders mattered in this world.

Equally important for me were the ceremonies, events, and topics of the conference that brought me back to my own childhood in St. Kitts. They allowed me to understand who I was, my place in the world, and where I could help Samoa and other islands. Yes, the flight connections I had to make to get there were long and arduous. But I began to understand that the connections to my earliest days were the most meaningful because they put, in a sense, all the separate elements of my own upbringing together.

At the conference, I began to recall how, shortly after my eleventh birthday, St. Kitts and Nevis gained their independence, on September 19, 1983. This period and all the years since this formative event in my life were exciting times. As a member of the youth mass choir and also one of the children in the independence parade, I was intimately involved in the preparations.

My class and, most likely, many other primary school students across the Federation of Saint Kitts and Nevis, were tasked with writing poems or drawing proposals for our national flag and coat of arms.

Though the memory of many of the specific events on that momentous day have faded, many aspects of my thinking and point of view were framed in that time of my life.

I joined the cadet corps two years later because my sense of national duty and fervor remained with me. Every year for Independence Day and Remembrance Day for soldiers killed in war, we had our parade. As a cadet, I was actively involved, marching and saluting the flag as our band played traditional and innovative tunes.

Another pivotal moment from my childhood had to do with my appreciation of nature.

At some point during these early years, before I was ten years old, my family spent a day in Nevis, and I remember my father driving a Mini Moke, a form of miniature jeep popular in the Caribbean at that time, with the rest of the family comfortably packed inside. We were seeking a friend of my parents who lived close to a water tank. I remember this because when we got lost, a young woman gave directions with quite colorful parlance as to where and how we could find the tank.

When we arrived at the home of the family friend, it was a sight to behold, with many beautiful fruit trees, flowers, and plants providing a natural landscape along the driveway and the garden.

The time of independence and the memories of nature on Nevis represent my youth; I have a romantic, whimsical longing for those days.

As I mentioned, my memories have become fewer and further apart through the progression of time. Yet, as fate would have it, in Samoa, after a journey to the other side of the world, I found an island very much like mine, and the memories came rushing back, much to my delight. And with the concepts of the conference to help me put things into perspective, I found it a truly transformative personal experience.

During those formative independence years, I read a book about islands of the Caribbean, the Pacific, and the South China Seas. This book marked the first time I became aware of the other islands out there. Samoa, in particular, struck me, and I wanted to know more. The tales helped build in me the desire to explore the world and to visit these islands somewhere beyond the seas. Thirty years would pass before I would set foot in Samoa. Not only did I finally explore this island I had read about as a child, but it was Samoa that seemed to bring me back to those wonderful days of my youth.

I had come to Samoa as one of the many participants at the Third International Conference on Small Island Developing States. After two years of preparations, we were finally here. Though I was on a professional visit to Samoa, the beauty of the island and absolute friendliness of its people took over.

From the minute we touched down at 2:00 a.m., we could feel the energy in the air; something special was taking place. The drive from the airport might have taken place in the middle of the night, but at every village along the way, there were signs and slogans welcoming all participants—every village. They took pride in their welcome and created very colorful visuals.

So why did Samoa bring back so many memories?

During the independence years of St. Kitts and Nevis, there was much hope for the future, a youthful enthusiasm for what was ahead. As our flag ascended and the national anthem was sung for the first time, we felt that everything from that moment would be possible for us.

Perhaps, as the world has gone through a great many changes over the last three decades, challenges have jaded the initial optimism. Island states have suffered from several global financial crises, frequent natural disasters, and the societal transformation these crises have engendered. Many of us felt the Third International Conference on Small Island Developing States would address these issues and bring back hope for the future of islands around the globe.

This would be the first time that a major international conference would be held in the Pacific Islands. Samoa had the chance to make history and be the pride of the region in guiding it. The people did not disappoint. When I arrived, what I witnessed was an expertly prepared island ready to showcase its beautiful culture and people.

As I drove around, I was genuinely pleased to see schoolchildren along our route, waving the flags of every island nation that had brought a delegation to the conference. As I observed this, I could not help but reflect on my own school class performing a similar exercise many years earlier.

Walking through the city center of Apia, I found everyone to be pleasant. If I paused for a second, appearing lost, someone was quickly there to show me the way.

Local television commercials kept welcoming the world to Samoa, and the news channels updated the country on any news about the conference. It was a true community affair, an island affair.

The cultural festival held for the conference also showcased the many aspects of Samoan life.

So why did this also have an impact on me? It might be common for global powers to put on such lavish affairs but not so a small island. Seeing a developing state such as Samoa rise to the occasion of giving us total, joyful immersion into their world, I was overcome. There had only been one other time when I had felt this, and that was during my childhood at the celebrations for the independence of St. Kitts and Nevis 30 years earlier.

I felt reborn in Samoa. The youthful vigor I thought I had lost and my hopes for a better tomorrow had returned. This feeling seemed to be shared by everyone around me.

St. Kitts and Nevis and Samoa are on different sides of the world. Our histories and cultures are not similar, yet I was home. I woke up early so that I could watch the sun rise over the mountain, and I traveled around the island, feeling that I was traveling between Cayon and Saddlers in St. Kitts, as the view seemed to be the same.

When I saw the homes filled with frangipani, banana trees, and coconut trees, my thoughts returned to that estate in Nevis. I had never found any place of its likeness until I came to Samoa. When I looked at the military parade, I was a cadet again, tapping out the drills in my head as the band marched by.

In addition to hosting the perfect international conference, Samoa also rekindled in me the promise of tomorrow.

To the young schoolchildren who welcomed us, I say, from one enthusiastic islander to another, "Fa'afetai tele mo lau talimalo fa'atamali'i ia te a'u i ou laufanua. O le lumana'i e fa'amoemoe i lau fa'atatau, ma e ausia mea uma pe 'a loto iai" (Thank you for welcoming me to your home. The future is as you will make it, and it is all possible).

Countryside of Samoa.

Chapter 4

EXPANDING THE ISLAND WAY: THE DIASPORA

Lambeth Town Hall in Brixton, London, England, close to Windrush Square, which was named in honor of the first wave of immigrants from the Caribbean who traveled to England on the HMT Empire Windrush. (Photo courtesy of Qais Yousef.)

In 1948, HMT *Empire Windrush* sailed from Jamaica to London, taking many Caribbean nationals to the United Kingdom in search of employment, following the end of the Second World War. These travelers and those who immediately followed became known as the *Windrush* generation, and they ushered in one of the largest waves of Caribbean migration to Europe and North America.

This period in Caribbean history has been showcased in literature, music, and television. One of the books read in Caribbean schools for a long time was the 1956 novel *The Lonely Londoners* by Trinidadian Samuel Selvon. It gave, in my view, a very good account of the challenges endured by some of these migrants. I still remember the cover page from one of the editions showing a lone man walking with his briefcase through the streets of London.

UB40, the reggae group, gave a fitting tribute to the *Windrush* generation in their music video to accompany their version of Lord Creator's "Kingston Town." I used to get reflective every time I saw it when I was younger, thinking of how brave it must have been to venture into the unknown with only the hopes of a better tomorrow as a guide.

A few of my aunts and uncles were members of a later wave of migrants to England. I once had a conversation with an uncle as to why he left the Caribbean and what his experience in England was like. His tale was one I will never forget.

He was a young man, all of 21 years of age, who had married my aunt and worked at the sugar factory in St. Kitts. He told me of the difficult conditions at the factory, where grown men would be beaten by the managers as though they were naughty children. It made it sting even more when he said that the managers were foreign nationals and all the abused staff were locals, as if replicating an earlier, more insidious colonial time.

He knew that he did not want his children growing up in this type of environment but was unsure of how best to remove himself from the situation. One day, while listening to the radio, he heard the voice of Winston Churchill saying, "Colonies, Mother England needs you."

This was a time when England encouraged immigration to fill the ranks of the labor force. My 21-year-old aunt and uncle discussed it and decided that my uncle would go first and make arrangements for the family to follow the next year.

The day came for him to set sail. He told me he watched the outline of St. Kitts fade into the distance, and I could only imagine that his heart did as well. The next day, when he awoke, he went on deck, and all around him there was only ocean, nothing else, as far as the eye could see. That moment brought the enormity of what he was doing into focus: he was traveling to the other side of the world, far away from the island home he knew and loved.

The year was difficult, sleeping in the cold, trying to find work, enduring racism and discrimination, and missing his family. But even through all his suffering, he was able to prepare for and provide for his family when they arrived.

The first migrants paved the way, and some made it easier for later generations of travelers. But they all had one thing in common: they never stopped pining for their island homes.

Now, if they pined for their island homes so much, why did they leave, you ask. But you already know the answer. Like most migrants, they searched for better opportunities, professionally and financially.

Because islands are small, with small populations and limited land, their economic sectors have not created opportunities for the multiple job seekers coming out of school. When my uncle left in the 1950s, he did not want to continue working in an environment where he faced the possibility of being disrespected and even abused. Additionally, the financial situation and limited job market made it difficult to forge a better life. The stories he heard of many jobs and financial opportunities overseas presented the option of working and sending money home. Many did this before opting to live permanently in these countries. The situation is different now, as the islands have made incredible advances, but the options and opportunities are still limited compared to much of the outside world.

A high school classmate wanted to study engineering, but he also wanted to remain in St. Kitts. When he completed his studies, he returned home to work, but there were no jobs for his specialty. He reluctantly left. Another colleague studied medicine and incurred very high student loans when he completed his residency. When he compared the options, he realized he would complete the repayment of his student loans in almost half the time if he stayed in North America.

These are the realities of islanders, but no matter where they roam, that island connection remains. When I was studying in Trinidad in the late 1990s, I would often visit a family friend in San Fernando. This lady had met my mother years earlier when my mother had been studying in Trinidad. They struck up a wonderful friendship that extended to both families, and I grew up calling her Aunt Enid. It's a common thing where I am from. As part of the wider family community of the islands, friends of our parents in the Caribbean were referred to as aunts and uncles. When I was in Trinidad, Aunt Enid ensured that I always had a place to call home, away from university accommodation, whenever I needed.

One weekend, while visiting Aunt Enid, I met a relative of hers who had just returned from living in Italy for the previous 30 years. This Trinidadian woman had traveled shortly after leaving high school and, eventually, settled in Italy. She found the country to be a lovely place and spent 30 years there teaching those she came in contact with about the Caribbean, our food, and our culture.

What struck me was the fact that even though she had spent more years of her life in Italy than in Trinidad, Trinidad was still home for her. She had not lost her accent, and she had been saving, through all of those years, to return home and live comfortably in retirement.

That is something I grew to understand about many of the island diaspora. Most, even those who don't return, pine for their island. Even those who are somewhat embarrassed about their island origins retain an interest in news about their island.

Islanders living overseas tune in to news from home. If their adopted city has a diaspora sufficiently large to warrant a visit from their home politicians, these islanders seek public meetings with their politicians so that they can express their views on developments at home.

So what is the impact of the diaspora for islanders? While not physically living on their islands, these islanders have kept the island way and even extended it to their adopted homes.

They have been instrumental in exporting island culture, and their impact has helped to show the outside world some of their great traditions. Whether it's the Cape Verdeans in Massachusetts, the Samoans in New Zealand, or the Grenadians in Toronto, the impact of the island diaspora has been felt.

I also studied at the University of Sussex in the Victorian beach resort city of Brighton, England, after I had completed my UWI education. I believe I was one of only three Caribbean students there at the time. However, we made sure our classmates and flatmates knew of our wonderful island experiences.

One day, one of my classmates rushed excitedly to tell me that there was a reggae club on the beach every Monday night. This was a club operated by Jamaicans playing the latest music from the Caribbean.

I doubted this, and when I went to investigate for myself, I was astonished to find that my classmate was correct. Some of these Jamaicans had been living in England for over 20 years, and they had not lost their "island flavor." There were others, I was told, who had been born in England and who sounded as though they had just left Jamaica. The music was, in fact, the latest from the Caribbean, and there were Caribbean drinks and food on occasion as well.

Many of the students who hailed from Europe, Asia, and Africa frequented this piece of Jamaica every Monday night, becoming a part of the island experience when they did.

In addition to the cultural connection, though, the island diaspora has, on occasion, become an influential constituent of the political scene.

The West Indian Day parade in Brooklyn on Labor Day has become an institution in the New York City annual calendar of events, and politicians make a point of coming out to campaign for votes, expressing their solidarity with island culture.

NEW YORK CITY: A MIGRANT'S CITY

I moved to New York City, first to represent St. Kitts and Nevis at the UN and, later, to work for the UN itself. While in New York, I connected with many of the St. Kitts and Nevis and Caribbean diaspora. I found that there was so much of an island community in the areas where our nationals settled that it was easier to have strong links and information from home. I could also enjoy delicacies from the bakeries and restaurants in those neighborhoods that were similar to those at home. Several of the churches that had predominantly Caribbean congregations assumed a style similar to the ones at home and became key areas for receptions, meetings, and fundraising activities for the islands.

Diaspora islanders used their island community spirit in New York and used their New York communities to help their island homes. People got together after hurricanes and raised money or collected items to send home to their families. Many sent home remittances quite regularly, which helped the welfare of their families at home, while others tried to convince the businesses in their neighborhoods to make donations to island causes.

Though, at times, the island diaspora's role has not been fully recognized, it remains a very important piece of the island way of life.

In New York City, itself a series of islands connected by bridges and tunnels, it is easy to find communities of migrants from all over the world. It is a great city with multicultural interactions taking place in every corner. This diversity also means even neighborhoods right next to each other will have a decidedly different feel. All of this is due to the ability of the migrants to recreate a sense of their homeland.

There are neighborhoods in the boroughs where the sounds, accents, music, and sights make you feel you have been transported to the country of their origin. When I am in New York and I miss the Caribbean, I head to Singh's Roti Shop in Queens for the ol' talk, the calypso, the doubles, and the vibe. I always leave feeling I have traveled back to the islands of the Caribbean.

But what is it about New York that has drawn so many immigrants? For many, it can be intimidating with its fast pace, aggression, and grit. It is easy to see why New Yorkers proudly proclaim their city to be Gotham. It also has an appeal that keeps anyone who has ever walked its streets addicted to its pull.

The music of the city is a microcosm of the world, with island music having as great an opportunity of pulling the crowds as any other genre on offer. My personal favorite is steel pan music, a product of Trinidad and Tobago, which has now become a popular form of entertainment among subway musicians. When I shift from one train to another on the major thoroughfares, my pace always changes once I hear the sounds of the city, and my walk falls into step with the beat of the music.

My favorite place in New York City is Central Park. You just never know what will happen while you are there. I remember strolling through the park on a summer day and, while walking over a bridge, I saw a group of people standing there with umbrellas. I thought it odd as there were no clouds, so I deduced it must be a theatrical performance. I paused to observe, along with many other passers-by.

Eventually, one of the umbrella carriers excitedly exclaimed, "They are coming!" and everyone ducked behind the wall of the bridge, holding their umbrellas up. We realised, then, that a marriage proposal was about to take place.

We looked out to the river and saw the couple sailing by in a gondola. The gondolier motioned to the group on the bridge to move to the other side, and they did, but a few who did not see him motion remained. That's when these New Yorkers became part of each other's stories.

We motioned to the stragglers that they needed to change sides and get back into formation. "Hurry!" we urged. This order was given to everyone. We could not risk any mistakes. Strangers stood there, directing each other to take up their proper formation. The woman with an "I" on her umbrella smiled at us as she hustled to her correct place.

Finally, they were ready. The gondolier had moved the boat to the other side and had turned it around. He gave a "thumbs up" gesture, and the umbrellas came out again.

The words, "Will you marry me?" beamed out from the bridge.

The man glanced up to make sure all was in place and gave the woman a piece of paper to read. She read, and what he wrote confused her. She looked at him and followed his gaze to the top of the bridge. While she exclaimed in shock, he reached into his pocket and produced the ring. She kissed him and took the ring. Then the umbrella handlers revealed themselves and clapped. All of the observers clapped as well. After all, this was also our moment.

The woman pointed to different people on the bridge, surprised to see people she knew, and shouted, "Grandma? You're here too?"

Her tears started to flow—just another New York City moment.

Although this was not a Caribbean, or island, experience, it helps to explain why so many islanders love New York. We feel that we are a part of that wider world we dreamed about when we lived on the islands.

Many Caribbean nationals of my generation enjoyed the movies and shows of the 1980s and 1990s that were based in New York. Once we arrive in New York, we try to visit every place we saw in those movies and television shows. For example, though not the most attractive experience, I can now relate fully to the E train that Prince Akeem boarded in *Coming to America*[9] when he chased his intended

---

9 Coming to America, directed by John Landis, produced by George Folsey Jr and Robert D Wachs, Paramount Pictures, 1988

to propose to her. But the Waldorf Astoria featured in that film, or the Roosevelt Island tram, featured in many other movies, both gave me that sense of satisfaction when I finally saw them. So when we can participate in that quintessential New York moment, like a proposal in Central Park, there is a certain "I have arrived" moment.

THE OTHER SIDE OF THE STORY

However, this "arrival" is superficial. There is a certain reality check that hits many from the diaspora community, which they don't speak of but perhaps should.

When the first generation of the island diaspora arrives, they assume that these great lands will welcome them with open arms and they will have access to the many things they saw or heard about when they lived on the islands. For many, this is not the case. In New York City, arriving at the top of the Empire State Building does not mean easily finding work on Wall Street or Broadway. Unfortunately, though, that is not the message that is sent back to the islands. Rather, the illusion of a better life outside continues.

I once had a conversation with a brilliant musician from the islands who was living in New York. He had left his island home for the opportunity to perform under the city's lights. He spoke of seeking jobs in order to survive while trying to make it and wanting to cry every winter when he thought of being on a beach back home.

He admitted to me that he regretted leaving, but when I asked him why he did not return to the islands, he replied, "Pride."

There is a belief that everything outside the islands must be better and those who left are looked upon with admiration, as they must, surely, be living the dream. The musician could not stomach returning and bursting the bubble of those at home who envied him for living abroad. He preferred to give the impression he was living better since he had left. Returning would be admitting failure and experiencing the disappointment of those at home.

It was amazing and difficult, in some ways, to comprehend. He knew that had he returned home, life would be better, and he could return to being that musical legend he had once been at a young age. But now, he preferred the façade of being better off because he lived in America.

The journey from the islands to Central Park or London, Toronto, Lisbon, Wellington, or Sydney is not an easy one. The media may show us how attractive these big cities are, and they may appear to be much more appealing than our own cities. Unfortunately, though, when we arrive, the welcome is not always the best, and sometimes this lingers through the generations.

Several children of Caribbean nationals have had a very difficult time in England. They were born in England and had little inter-action with their island homes, save for their parents' stories. They thought of themselves as British but found that, on several occasions, they were not considered British by other British nationals; they were referred to as Caribbean nationals.

I have seen some of them become very angry and lost even, not wanting to be considered from the islands as though this were a bad thing. I associated this with the shame that some islanders felt and that, perhaps, had passed down to their children. But their feelings were also influenced by the prevailing negativism in these large cities where islanders have been looked down on and marginalized. The children, then, in an attempt to be accepted, disassociate themselves from their island heritage. So it seemed that the same attitude that was directed toward islanders also extended to the children of island migrants. Such sentiments transcended borders and generations.

For the diaspora community, it is a choice as to whether to stay outside or return home. Like many migrants, some are successful while others are not. For many in the island diaspora, however, the connection remains. Those of us who are not ashamed of where we are from try to replicate the islands in our adopted homes. I saw this among the Dominicans, another of the significant diaspora communities in New York.

A NIGHT ON THE TOWN
WITH DOMINICANS

Another New York City parade that is part of the city tradition is the Dominican Day Parade where the people of the Dominican Republic showcase their culture. Dominicans now represent one of the very largest immigrant ethnic groups in New York, with estimated numbers of 600,000, making them a significant force even in a city of over eight million residents. Traveling to a Dominican neighbourhood in New York can feel like a trip to the Dominican Republic itself due to the strong maintenance of traditions. I decided to embark on this journey to get a sense of the Dominican lifestyle and also to use this experience as an example of how the island diaspora nurtures and exports its culture.

181ST STREET

181st Street, Washington Heights, New York City.

The New York City subway is, probably, the fastest way to link all of the New York City communities, as long as it is working well. So this was going to be my means of transport to the Dominican community.

Islanders are not traditional fans of the subway system. The subway represents everything we are not: it is often crowded, the space is cramped, and the bulk of the commute is underground. If you are from an island with wide-open spaces, countless outdoor activities, and the beach as your getaway, you will find the subway to be a bit of a challenge. But like all New Yorkers, we make do. We suck it up, prepare for the crowds, and venture forth.

The place where you can find a large community of Dominicans is West 181st Street, in Washington Heights. The moment I exited the subway, I felt I was the only non-Dominican around, as everyone else spoke Spanish. One gentleman in front of me sang all the way from the subway car to the street, oblivious to everyone around him as his voice boomed out a Spanish tune.

On the street, I looked around and knew I had been transported to Santo Domingo. On every street corner, the vendors stood selling *pastelitos*, which were the same meat-filled patties we ate throughout the English-speaking Caribbean. The local supermarkets had sections for local produce and island imports, bringing the taste of the Dominican Republic to upper Manhattan. Looking at this, I was reminded of the markets in Fiji, Samoa, and the Seychelles.

As I walked around, the streets were alive with the music of the Dominican Republic. I have often marveled at the differences in the beat, yet resemblances in the sounds, of island music. I initially thought that the Dominican Republic and Cuba had similar music to the British Caribbean because we were in the same region, yet I heard similar rhythms in Samoa as well. It is not about regions but has to do with the fact that we are all from islands.

Several of the streets in Washington Heights had been renamed in honor of Dominican national heroes to ensure the next generation would understand the cultural legacy of those who had come before.

Dominicans in New York City have made quite an impact. The Dominican Day Parade, held each August, is a major highlight on the city's festival calendar, with the national colors and pride being displayed all down Sixth Avenue. All year round, politicians of Dominican descent make their presence felt on the American landscape.

But like most islanders, there remains a connection to all that occurs back home, both in conversation and through frequent visits to family. On West 181st Street, you often see men standing on the sidewalk discussing their island's politics. They have eyes on both the island and the continent, keeping the link between the two alive.

Spending time in Washington Heights in the Dominican community helped me to connect to its culture. The similarities between the other migrant islanders prevailed and showed how important the diaspora was to the continued preservation of the culture and heritage of the islands.

Chapter 5

ISLAND IMPACTS: ADVERSITY AND THE ENDURING LEGACY OF BOB MARLEY

"Bob Marley," cast bronze by Alvin Marriott, Celebrity Park, Kingston, Jamaica. (Photo courtesy of Sheree Chambers.)

I once had a conversation with a gentleman from the Solomon Islands in the South Pacific who told me a tale about the challenges his people endured as they tried to complete their education. There are many islands that make up the sovereign country of the Solomon

Islands, he said, and access to education is difficult. All of the islands have primary schools, but not all of them have high schools. Students on those islands must head to high school on another island by boat.

This gentleman said that when he was growing up, scholarships were often only available each year to the top two students in each primary school. This was also the situation in the secondary schools where only the top two to three would go on to university, which was either in Australia, Fiji, or New Zealand. The lack of funds and the high cost of education meant only a fortunate few would get there.

This story had a profound impact on me because I was familiar with people back home who had to travel to another island by boat for secondary education. Both of my parents did this. I also knew others for whom this was too great an obstacle; they were unable to receive further education because of the distance and the finances. I knew what became of such people with limited means and wondered what happened to students on the Solomon Islands who finished third or fourth in their class. What opportunities were in place for them?

I know from personal experience islanders are very resilient, and when I heard this tale, I grew curious about the Solomon Islanders. The country has been trying to make educational access easier, but has it worked out? For those without access to higher education, what alternatives are there?

If you are also an islander, you might want to ask yourself some of these same questions. Is your island similar to those I have visited or completely different? Is your diaspora as impactful in preserving your culture and exporting your heritage as the Dominican diaspora is? How similar are your challenges to those of the people from my country, St. Kitts and Nevis?

At times, when I look at the challenges that islanders' face, particularly in having their voices heard around the world, the situation may seem hopeless. But one of the things I have observed is how much the success of one islander means to others.

The West Indies cricket team was a beacon of hope for many Pacific Islanders, who saw within this team hopes for their own island dreams, even half a world away. When Sir William Arthur Lewis, a native of St. Lucia, gained international prominence for his economic theories and won the Nobel Prize, islanders across the world beamed in pride. It sent a message that those of us from even the tiniest, most seemingly obscure places could also achieve this level of success around the world, while not forgetting where we came from.

But how far can we truly reach? Indeed, the impact of islanders can be global. I would find this power of other islanders on my trips, sometimes when I was at a low point and needed it most to connect me, creating a sense of clarity. This came for me on a trip to Qatar, in the Middle East, for an international meeting. And it was there that I came to terms with perhaps the most famous and successful islander of them all, Bob Marley. Like a vision of the Virgin Mary to someone who believes in religious signs, hearing him on the radio at just the right moment gave me clarity and purpose, connected me to my homeland, and provided the strength I needed to stay resilient in a challenging situation.

The Trip to Qatar

As you no doubt have guessed, I love to travel. There was a time—and to an extent, the feelings are still there—when, if you told me, "Let's take a trip to that place you've never been on the other side of the world," I would already have a mental picture of what I would be packing and would look at you expectantly to learn how soon we would be going. Yet early on, as much as I enjoyed going halfway around the world to a new place, many of my closest friends thought I was strange for such desires. Many early acquaintances seemed not to desire venturing far from home. At times, some even questioned why I wanted to travel, as if I were telling them home was not good enough. Of course, this was before I actually traveled and met a world of like-minded souls who also loved to travel and explore.

It was therefore a surprise to many people when I said no to a trip to Qatar. The reality is I had already been there before. I loved it and found it beautiful, but the trip left me ambivalent. It was, after all, a place where customs officials had not recognized the existence of my country.

The meeting in Qatar was the UN Framework Convention on Climate Change (UNFCCC). This was not one that I was particularly eager to attend, and the fact it would last for two weeks played into my apprehensions. If you want to witness an occasion of difficult negotiations, constant accusations, stalling tactics, and frustration, a climate change meeting would be the place for you.

It was frustrating because this is an important issue, not just for islands but for every country. But in my view, too many countries either delay progress or remain unconvinced that climate change is a real threat. The thought of sitting through this rhetoric, once again, for another two weeks, with very little concrete action accomplished, was not my idea of working to save the islands. In addition, I was not a climate change expert, which did not make me the best fit for this type of meeting. I fear that, unfortunately, each incremental advance made at the UNFCCC meetings is much slower than climate change itself.

So I was reluctant to travel to Qatar on this occasion, even as the representative of St. Kitts and Nevis on such an important issue. There was another reason for my not wanting to travel at that time. I was preparing for an interview to work at the UN on small island developing states issues. This was the job I truly wanted. The UN was the place where I believed I could do more good for the islands than as a delegate at a climate change meeting. All I could think about that week was the journey from being a student with eyes wide open in 1994 during the Barbados meeting to being an idealistic government representative in 2005 in Mauritius. This UN job would bring the process full circle for planning the Third International Conference on Small Island Developing States. It was a thrill to think I might be working for the UN, that organization upon which a great many islanders had pinned their hopes.

This was the job I needed. It would change many aspects of my professional and personal life. Perhaps, it is never a good idea to place so much on one job, but this was the one for me. I did not want to jeopardize this opportunity by missing out on the interview.

The interview was scheduled for a Friday. Fortunately, it was a telephone interview, and the interviewers were willing to make the call to Qatar. Nevertheless, the disruption caused by having to travel while preparing for the interview was annoying.

I protested and asked if I could delay my visit to Qatar until the following week. My role in delivering the national statement was not required until then, in any event, so I would not forsake my duties. I was advised, however, that no one else would be attending and that it was very important that someone from St. Kitts and Nevis deliver the statement at the UNFCCC. So off to Qatar I ventured. The full travel time was 27 hours, and I would have another 16 before the interview. Not ideal, but I could do this. I would do this. The opportunity would not be lost.

When I arrived in Qatar, the greeting was not ideal. The customs staff had not updated their records for St. Kitts and Nevis from my last visit, meaning that my nation was still not in their database. Beyond that, the person who was to have greeted me at the airport to take me to the hotel was not there.

I knew that this was one of the indignities that islanders and others from obscure parts of the world face all the time. The very disturbing process, which included being detained and interrogated for two hours, reflected the challenge that we islanders face in striving for some form of acknowledgement that we do, in fact, exist. After traveling for more than a day, I felt I might be at the breaking point. Was I not a professional, representing my own country, just as most other passengers at the airport were doing on that night?

It would not be the last indignity I suffered. I would find out that my own colleagues had betrayed me. Headquarters had sent someone else in addition to me, someone who would take precedence over me. He would be the one to deliver the statement. Unbeknownst to me, he had even been on one of my flight connections. I wondered whether the greeter was there for him instead of me.

What was I to think? Perhaps it was the pressure of the interview, the harassment of travel, or the deception I perceived, but I was not in a happy place. I was in a rage, pure unadulterated rage. I did not know how I would react when we encountered each other, but I did not care. I would let my displeasure be known.

At that point, I needed air. The hotel room was suffocating, and I felt like a caged animal. I left the compound, wanting to go anywhere. I did not care where, just far enough away.

THE BOB MARLEY MOMENT

I hailed a taxi, hoping to get as far away from my thoughts and the hotel as possible, even if briefly. And that was when it hit me. As I got into the taxi, still seething, I was greeted by the voice of Bob Marley singing, of all things, "Every little thing's gonna be all right."[10]

I was nearly stupefied. I looked at the smiling driver and asked, "Where are you from?"

"Eritrea," was his reply. I was surprised to find someone from the small East African nation there.

"You like this music, do you?" I asked.

"I grew up on this. I love Bob Marley."

We drove on in silence as I sat back and listened to this hypnotic messenger from the past and found myself overcome with emotion. My moment of clarity had arrived. My anger had dissipated, and I looked outside at the city of Doha, Qatar's capital. Too consumed with other matters, I had forgotten how beautiful it was. I started to reflect on all that was good and believed, truly believed, that everything would be all right.

THE SIGNIFICANCE OF BOB MARLEY

I once had a conversation about Bob Marley with an Australian aborigine. She told me that many aborigine youth who had learned

---

10 Marley, Robert, "Three Little Birds," *Exodus*, 1977.

to play the guitar, learned the instrument by playing Bob Marley's "Redemption Song" because of its significance for them.

One can only hope that Bob knew of the impact he had far beyond his island shores. He started singing of his island reality and got the world singing about "a government yard in Trench town."[11] But he did not stop there. He looked around the world and, like many islanders, reflected on issues of international concern, sometimes being one of the earliest to do so. This islander got the world singing his messages.

For many us from the Caribbean, Bob Marley is an institution. Most, if not all, Caribbean households have at least one Bob Marley recording. Every year, on his birthday and anniversary of his death, his music plays on the radio stations across the region. Whenever there are local shows, all the performer has to do is channel Bob, and the crowd is soothed.

His children have the blessing and the curse of having his name. We celebrate them as our link to him, but we are disappointed because they are not him. When Rita, his wife, intimated a desire to take his remains to Ethiopia, there was a public outcry. "No! He belongs to us!"

But in reality, to whom does Bob Marley belong?

Growing up, I knew of people from the inner cities who did not want middle-class, and definitely not upper-class, Caribbean people listening to his music. "He spoke to us and for us, not for you," they would shout angrily to any others enjoying the music.

West Indians look with curiosity at anyone from outside the Caribbean who enjoys Marley's music. I was at a reception where one of his songs was playing in the background. An older lady from

---

11 Bob Marley and the Wailers, "No Woman No Cry," *Natty Dread*, 1974.

Southern Africa sang along. My younger, naïve self, asked quite foolishly, "How do you know this music?" Well, she rightly put me in my place. "You Caribbean people always believe Bob Marley belongs only to you. He belongs to us all. I was at university when he performed in Zimbabwe. I did not know how I would get to see him, but I was determined. So my friends and I took a bus, a train, and walked for miles across Africa to see him."

I can't compete with that. I never saw him perform live, and I certainly did not travel across a continent to see him. I can say this, though. On that day in Qatar, I needed to hear him, and I did. I knew nothing else about my taxi driver, but we bonded over an appreciation of the power of Bob's words and music. The driver seemed to know that I had transitioned through different emotions during that drive. He played another Marley song for good measure before wishing me a good day.

For the rest of that day I was in a state of total calm. I remember drinking some amazing Moroccan tea while observing the culture of the Persian Gulf all around me. I spent the day admiring dhows—ancient sailing vessels—in the harbor, the Emiri Diwan Palace, and other buildings that are the architectural splendor of the city. Meanwhile, the 2030 National Vision program for the country, complete with billboards all around the city, was very inspiring.

When I eventually encountered the colleague who had been sent along on the trip with me, he was uncomfortable at first, unsure, I imagine, of how I would react. But I no longer held any malice; everything was going to be all right. It showed on my face, and I felt it in my heart.

And everything was, in fact, all right. I was selected for the job I had interviewed for, completing a 15-year professional odyssey and allowing me to experience even more island moments with the UN.

FLEETING CLARITY

When I left Qatar, I had another slightly irritating experience as, once again, I was interrogated for an hour over my "nonexistent" country. My internal pleasure was to not purchase any Qatari trinkets on my way out. Take that Qatar! You will not steal my joy. Everything was still going to be all right.

However, I did channel some of the revolutionary Bob at that point because I declared then and there not to return to Qatar until the customs officials learned to treat all people with respect, no matter where they were from. Qatar hopes to become a global player with respect to hosting many international events, so it should beware. I may not be the only one aggrieved.

IMPACTS

Bob Marley was an islander of humble beginnings who had a global reach. He showed just how far islanders could dream and also that they do not have to forget from whence they hail. Islanders can show the world the greatness of their own particular culture and allow the world to celebrate it with them.

We can be intellectual innovators like Sir Arthur Lewis or international leaders like Dr. Carlos Lopes of Guinea Bissau who became head of the UN Economic Commission for Africa. Many young basketball players in the Caribbean look at Tim Duncan as a role model, a man who came from an island and went on to dominate the National Basketball Association. Meanwhile, the singer Lura, the daughter of Cape Verdean parents living in Portugal, has continued to inspire many with her island-style music.

Island impacts can go far. These famous islanders and many unsung others tailored their work ethic, theories, or themes on their island homes or heritage, and showed the world just how great they and, by extension, their islands could be.

In essence, those of us from the islands, venturing far from our homelands, can all be as impactful as Bob Marley.

Chapter 6

FACING THE STORM TOGETHER AS A COMMUNITY

Annual weather patterns are natural occurrences around the world. We plan our festivals and activities by these patterns and for the most part can prepare for what is to come from experience. Despite its being a hackneyed topic, the weather still remains a popular way to break the ice in any conversation.

I have ruminated on global conversations about the weather that regularly focus on certain areas while ignoring other areas. For me, this was no more real than the difference in reactions to severe weather activity in certain metropolitan cities and in the islands.

For example, there is a global appeal about New York, brought on by the many comic books, novels, songs, television shows, and films. If a blizzard is approaching New York City, the world stops to see what's going on. Even when I did not live there, I followed the path of a storm to the city that never sleeps, hopeful that all would be well. At the time, I had not witnessed snow up close, but I almost felt I knew what New Yorkers were going through by watching the cable news or looking at stories on the Internet.

By now, I've experienced several snow storms in New York City, including Winter Storm Juno of 2015 and the Polar Vortex of 2014. During both those occurrences, I received many enquiries from friends and acquaintances in the Caribbean, Latin America, Europe, India, and Africa as to how I was managing. I remember watching the Australian Open during a storm in New York, and while they showed the images of beautiful Melbourne in the summertime, the ESPN commentators kept apologizing to the New York City viewers and asked us to post images of the snow for other viewers around the world to see what we were experiencing.

It was during this time that I thought about the lack of global, or sometimes even regional, coverage of severe weather on an island. The reality hit me that unless people have actually experienced one of these storms and have some connection to the island that is being struck by such a storm, they do not have much interest in it. I myself, while being fully cognizant of most of the hurricanes that have hit the United States over the last decade, have limited knowledge of which storms hit the Pacific Islands during that same period.

I must say, though, that in March 2015, when Cyclone Pam devastated Vanuatu, the BBC brought it up close and personal to viewers across the globe. I sat, for the first time while in New York, and saw the damage hours after it had occurred on an island halfway around the world. I was very grateful to the BBC for this. Hopefully, such coverage will help to sensitize people to the plight of islands when disaster strikes.

I fully appreciate the importance of highlighting the challenges faced by those affected by blizzards. My hope is that this interest can focus on the islands as well, because I often wonder to what extent non-islanders are aware of the impact of storms on small islands.

The first hurricane I experienced was Hurricane Hugo. This storm wreaked havoc across the Caribbean in September 1989, and for those of us who faced it, the memories are still alive. Fear of storms and rallying to help each other are shared island experiences.

Before that powerful storm St. Kitts and Nevis had not recently had a severe hurricane. Quite a few of us did not fully appreciate the extent of a hurricane's impact.

The week before the storm, the weather was beautiful, balmy tropical, with clear skies and gentle breezes. The island's mango trees were soon to be harvested of their delightful fruits, and they were some of the sweetest I had tasted in years. I had been waiting with anticipation for the third crop of the season to be ready in approximately two weeks.

The news stations warned of the formation of the storm, but most of us scoffed. Over the previous decade the hurricanes had either petered out or turned north before they made landfall. This would do the same. We were special and protected.

The day before the storm was due to arrive, it became extremely hot, hotter than I could remember. There was no wind anywhere. This was strange, as the ocean breeze is a constant on an island.

Despite this, nobody was carrying out much preparation. We knew what to do. The older people had drilled it into our heads for years, so we did it automatically: filled our pots and buckets with water; made sure the lamps and lanterns had enough oil; brought out the candles and matches; and turned the fridge to the coldest setting so that the food would not spoil as quickly. Once all of this was done, we just had to wait patiently until the storm passed.

This would just be another opportunity for family bonding, for storytelling and quiet reflection as a little bit of rain and wind blew outside.

Nothing to worry about.

That evening, the darkest clouds we had ever seen started rolling across the ocean toward us. "What is that?" many wondered. "We'd better get indoors."

The winds came next, very gradually, puffs at first, every ten minutes or so, and then, heavier gusts, much more frequently. The trees started rustling more and more violently, and we could hear the remaining mangoes and other objects slamming against the walls outside. It was unsettling.

As the hours passed, the hurricane grew more and more ferocious. This first part occurred during the night, and we tried to sleep, but it was an uneasy task.

I don't remember when we lost electricity, but I know I was grateful for sunlight so that we could see what was really taking place outside. My mother and I stood at one of the windows and looked out at our neighbors' homes. A few roofs looked as if they would not last the storm. We hoped the inhabitants would be okay. If necessary, we would assist them.

Suddenly, we heard a creaking sound. We looked at each other, confused, and then we looked up. The corner of the roof was starting to lift.

Many of the homes back then had roofs made of galvanized steel and wood. When it rained, we would have the occasional leak and would seal the hole when the rains had passed. But seeing the galvanized roof rise meant trouble. If the wind got underneath, there was nothing to protect us from the elements.

Fortunately, we had a lower level, and we sounded the alarm for everyone to move essentials below. We hustled. The creaking got louder, which meant we did not have much time left. My sister was nine years old at the time, and I remember her picking up her pet kitten with one hand and her favorite books and a lamp in the other.

I would like to believe it was divine guidance that we were all at the lower level, just about to make another run upstairs to secure our belongings, when an excruciating rumbling sound bellowed above us. Out of nowhere, bricks and large pieces of wood came crashing down a few feet from where we stood. My eyes opened wide. I could not believe what was taking place.

The water followed in quick succession. This was more than rain. It flooded down as if buckets were being poured out on us. It was also icy cold, which I thought very strange for the tropics.

We could not stand around for long, as we had to try and secure everything at risk from the water.

Finally, all we could do was sit with our feet up or lie on the beds. They, at least, were protected, but all around us ice-cold water gushed through the house.

If the waters kept rising, we would have to vacate, but we were uncertain about where we could flee. On a small island, when a hurricane comes, it affects almost everywhere. We had already heard, before the radio station was destroyed, that our nearest storm shelter had lost its roof as well, so that was no longer an option. We spent the rest of the day with this uncertainty on our minds, but fortunately, we did not have to run into the elements to safety.

As traumatic as this was for us, there were many who had worse experiences. One of my neighbors had to find shelter in a clothes closet until the storm passed, as this was the only place where her head could remain dry. She stood there for hours.

There was also the woman who had to give birth by candlelight, as the stories circulating the island after the storm claimed. The tale must be true because she named her son Hugo in honor of the storm.

The island community spirit emerged fast. Within hours of the passage of the hurricane, many people reached out to us. Two of our neighbors, who had been walking around surveying the damage, came to our aid as we tried to salvage what we could. The news spread, and many more came to help. My father, a historian, had many documents and books that were no longer in print. It would have been quite unfortunate to have lost them, some of which he had been collecting for decades. Another neighbor went to work, quickly drying the books. She was able to save most of them due to her fast action.

It was difficult for my siblings, who were studying in New York and Washington, DC at the time. They had no idea what was taking place, as all communication with the island was down. This was also where media coverage would have helped. People outside the island only knew of the storm because members of the diaspora were frantically trying to get in touch with their relatives. Word reached them a few days later that the family home had been damaged. I could imagine their concern, not knowing our fate while learning of the damage to the house. It would be a week before they received word that we were okay.

One day, a gentleman came to look for us. He owned a ham radio, which allowed him to speak to anyone who had a similar device. He connected with someone who lived in the same neighborhood in New York City as my eldest sister did. Somehow, he found my sister, and we could finally speak with her. It had been weeks since we had spoken, but the conversation helped assure us that all would soon return to normal and we would recover from the storm.

As the years have passed, the islands have faced much more frequent and severe storms. We are definitely not cavalier about them anymore and go into full survival mode when the season begins each year from July on.

But the reality is that, despite our preparations, islands are at risk, and many islanders are affected each year when the storms arrive. I know of people who have had to be evacuated by boat from their homes because the area has flooded. Others have had to send their children to neighboring islands to complete their education because their homes and schools have been destroyed. We try to build stronger houses, but this is a challenge, as these storms are becoming increasingly severe.

Nevertheless, we rebuild. These are our homes, and though, at times, the challenge is great, we do have the wider island community and diaspora to reassure us that these trials will not be borne alone.

However, there are times when we don't feel the support within the wider global community. I once sat in a room with people from all over the world, including many islanders, when a gentleman remarked, "Why should we feel sorry for the islands just because they are weak and vulnerable?"

He was reacting to the suggestion by islanders that the use of fossil fuels may have had an impact on the increase in climate change. I was flabbergasted. Yes, islands are severely affected by the rising sea level, flooding, ocean acidification, and storms. But I was of the view that so too were many other countries, including the great powers. The effects on these areas might, perhaps, be less severe or not as visible. Still, my thoughts in that conversation were that a global effort should be made to see how this issue could be addressed.

I know that gentleman viewed the suggestion of the fossil fuel link as a threat to his profit margin, but his contention that islands were weak and vulnerable and therefore did not merit his sympathy was quite unfortunate in a global community.

All of us from these remote dots in the oceans of the world know that the size of our islands presents a challenge in adjusting to phenomena linked to climate change. Islands are more susceptible to shocks, but islanders are neither weak nor vulnerable. We definitely have never sought anyone's pity. Rather, we are resilient and continue to face the storms. We have always been appreciative of those who assist, and we do try to offer advice from lessons learned, even to those who deem us weak and think that they themselves won't have to, one day, face the wrath of the storms that we currently face.

Chapter 7

REFLECTIONS ON THE PRESENT
AND FUTURE OF ISLANDS

Basseterre, St. Kitts. (Photo courtesy of Marissa Richardson.)

W hen I was leaving my island home in 2001 to work at the
Permanent Mission of St. Kitts and Nevis to the UN in New
York, I took a drive around the country before traveling. That cir-
cumnavigation lasted all of four hours, and even that was because I
stopped at various spots along the way. My island home is, after all,

just a few miles across from one end to the other. I wanted to remind myself of those for whom I was going to advocate at the UN. I saw fishermen who were going through a rough patch because they were competing with larger fishing vessels from countries far away. The local fisher folks' boats, nets, and other equipment were no match for the more technologically advanced vessels and equipment of the foreigners.

So those memories of the conch shell being blown as the boats came back from a day at sea, to a large extent, were all we had of the local custom, just memories.

I saw workers in the sugar industry who were facing an uncertain future because the trade was on its last legs after three centuries of being the main economic activity in the country.

I wanted to make a positive difference in their lives. "Their causes will be mine," I told myself, "and I will help to change the tide of challenges that they face."

So young and naïve I was for thinking I could go into that great big world and shout louder than all of the other voices that were already shouting and who had the advantage of size, influence, and a support base. How could I make my island's issues relevant?

The first step to promoting that relevance was the realization that there were many other islands out there with similar experiences and challenges. Understanding that there was, indeed, an "island way" became almost cathartic for me. It helped me to appreciate my island culture and heritage even more.

My island exploration since that first trip to the UN was educational, entertaining, and eye opening. I confess that before taking the international trips through other islands during 2013 and 2014, I thought I already understood island life. I did, in actuality, but my point of reference had been my own island. After those journeys, there were some observations that I probably would not have made had I not traveled.

First, reggae music is universal. As I moved around Fiji, Samoa, and the Seychelles, the reggae beat followed me. I heard songs I grew up on in the Caribbean and those that were currently making the airwaves, playing on the radios and televisions of the Pacific and the Indian Ocean. I expected this in Jamaica, naturally, but as I walked around a local arts and craft store in Fiji, a poster of Bob Marley greeted me while Peter Tosh played on the radio. In the Seychelles, while having a meal of barbecued delicacies on the beach one afternoon, I commented to the bartender that the music was very soothing to me, as a West Indian. He smiled a broad smile and replied, "We love our reggae here as well."

Similarly, while I enjoyed a relaxing afternoon among members of the Cape Verdean diaspora living in Massachusetts, reggae dominated the background sound.

What this showed me was that island culture has the ability and capacity to influence the world. We did have a cross-island link of reggae music and even Rastafarianism, but at my reggae club on the beach in Brighton, a great many Europeans with dreadlocks enjoyed the music and sang of the experiences of the Jamaicans.

Second, the island diaspora is an integral part of the island way of life. Rather than viewing migrants as people who "fled" or "abandoned" the islands or, for that matter, as people who are better off than those they left behind, we should acknowledge their roles and their connections to the islands. The islands are beautiful places that explain so much more about the second and third generations of migrants than they, or anyone else for that matter, realize.

Having taken this trip, I know that island travel is not easy because of the vast distance and time required for the journeys. Islanders must undertake extensive planning when they want to travel to other islands, especially if the islands are in different regions. But we have so much to learn from each other and to offer the world.

Island culture has evolved into an important part of island societies. I have heard the suggestion that culture should be a pillar of sustainable development for the islands. But the culture of many islanders is unknown to many people not intimately connected to those particular islands.

We are beautiful people with an identity, the identity of the islander. And no matter where we roam, this is our pride.

As a result of these journeys, I felt more connected to islands everywhere. It is my hope that this snapshot of island culture and island people brings more attention to islands. Whether islands are viewed as sources of fun, sun, and sand or whether people have only a marginal interest in them, I hope a deeper understanding of the people and their joys and challenges will afford a better appreciation of what it means to be an islander. I hope that islanders will gain a sense of pride for who they are and where they come from.

We have made important contributions to the global community in entertainment, sports, politics, academia, international affairs, and much more. Some of these contributions came from our island experiences, which allowed us to present a different perspective in discussions.

Sometimes, we are not aware of the impact we've had on the world, but we give our best shot at making that impact.

So when Samoans show they can host a top-class global event or St. Lucians show they can produce two Nobel Laureates in completely different fields from a population of 174,000 or when Sidney Poitier won the Best Actor award at the Academy of Motion Pictures, they all become sources of pride for islanders and reasons to celebrate the islands.

The island experience is not just for islanders, though. Tourism is important to the islands, but venturing off the traditional tourist path and becoming a part of the island way of life can help to expand that awareness and bring a deeper appreciation of island people.

There is also a certain innocence to growing up on an island. A cocoon, almost, an island is created by the very waters that surround it and makes its people cling to their society, which has grown into extended families and imbued them with an intense love of their land. We love and are in awe of the ocean, and we have a relaxed mind-set. I've often wondered if the waves take away negativity and tension and leave peace of mind in their place.

We also, for the most part, love to travel. This probably comes from the fact that after a certain amount of time, we have seen all there is to see on our island, and the limitless human spirit wants more. But even when we travel and reflect on that island flavor, it soothes something inside us and makes us yearn for that afternoon on the beach or for those moments when the island breeze caresses our face.

I understand why tropical islands are sometimes considered paradise. As a native islander, I feel and believe in this sentiment. I never tire of the notion now.

But even though islands seem to be paradise, we islanders have our challenges. Because our economies are small and open, we are heavily affected by any fizzle in the international economy. Unfortunately, when economists speak globally, they do not take into account the small populations of islands and the fact that a "minor glitch" in world economic growth can be an economic calamity for 100,000 people or fewer living on an island. Competition between global powers over terms of trade is a catastrophe for island communities.

Additionally, surrounded by water, we are at the front lines of climate change. We experience the rising sea level up close and personal, and when a disaster strikes, it strikes us very hard.

But we persevere. We are resilient, because this is our home, and we want nothing but the best for it.

We love deeply, we love strongly, and we love honestly, but we are, sometimes, suspicious of outsiders out of fear of losing our lands, our culture, or ourselves. We have, after all, experienced such losses time and time again through colonial invasions and oppression, none of which are distant memories.

In spite of this, we love to experience other cultures and to compare them to our own. We love and appreciate what the outside world has to offer, but we also want our culture and our way of life to be appreciated.

Jamaicans have an expression, "Wi lickle but wi tallawah," which, basically, translates as "Islands are small but more powerful than they appear." Islanders tend to punch above their weight because they need to be heard and felt. That is a reaction to the indifference some have exhibited to islanders. Islanders are never content to be considered small and on the margins of what goes on in the world. Many islanders want to be in the midst of everything that is happening, and all islanders want the world to recognize their contributions.

As a final analysis, islanders only want to be respected for who and what they are: a beautiful people with much to add to the world.

My island journeys awakened in me a renewed love of the islands and a desire to learn more. They also made me want to do more to help my fellow islanders. The outside world does not always understand islands, and an islander can help to bridge that gap. I hope I can continue to be one of those bridge builders. Additionally, as an islander, I want to join other islanders, working together and in partnership with non-islanders to provide those valuable resources required to build resilience on the islands. I know that our people are the most critical factors of our development, and if we can tap into the potential of the islands, we can accomplish great things. This realization grew in me by leaps and bounds once I embraced the island way of life.

My voyage of exploration was just the beginning. There are many more islands to visit and islanders to meet. With each one, I look forward to learning a little bit more about myself and a whole lot more about other islands and the wonderful impact that islanders can make.

Hopefully, this will be a journey experienced by many others as well.

View of Nevis from the Southeast Peninsular, St. Kitts.

ADDENDUM

A Photo Journal of the Islands

No trip throughout the islands is complete without beholding the visual delights. These are a few of my favorite images taken during my island journeys.

I have also pointed out in this book the importance of some of these images beyond the visual. Many highlight the need to preserve both the natural and the man-made wonders of these islands. Through sustainable development, these beautiful sites and cultural customs can continue to hold economic importance for locals for centuries through tourism, agriculture, and many other industries.

PRESERVING THE ENVIRONMENT AND CULTURE

Preserving the environment is not an endeavor unique to islanders. Fortunately, more and more people around the world understand the importance of environmental preservation, and it is discussed at every level. However, there is still a need for more people to understand how significant it is.

My first Earth Day celebration took place when I was in primary school and my class planted a tree. That simple exercise has remained with me all these years later and has helped to shape my thinking about the environment, especially when I attended the Rio+20 Conference on Sustainable Development in 2012. I felt it was essential that there was an understanding among as many persons as possible, from world leaders to the youngest of students, about caring for our home.

The Sleeping Giant in Fiji.

Fiji and the Seychelles have different ways of preserving the environment. A nature reserve such as the Garden of the Sleeping Giant and the sustainable development of Victoria, the capital of the Seychelles, reaffirmed in me that islanders were also playing their part in this weighty issue.

Victoria, capital of the Seychelles, on the island of Mahé.

When I was in Samoa, I took a tour of the Piula Cave Pool. We had a good laugh while taking in the sites. It was as if I were driving around my own island or any island in the Caribbean. Samoa and the Caribbean islands are that much alike.

Samoa was the first place where I had seen coconut trees growing in the mountains—at least, as far as I can remember. Coconut trees are normally close to the ocean and the beaches, but in Samoa, plantations of these trees extended far into the sky. No wonder I could have coconuts every morning for breakfast and coconut water all day.

A few of us were a bit tentative about going into the cold water of the pool, and we were unsure of how deep it was. My friend Isabelle had no such qualms. In she jumped, putting the rest of us to shame. Then she swam into the cave to take a picture of one of the best views in Samoa.

Piula Cave Pool, Samoa. (Photo courtesy of Isabelle Mckusick.)

Green vervet monkey in St. Kitts. (Photo courtesy of Sally Richardson.)

In St. Kitts and Nevis, the green vervet monkey has become a much more visible sight than in previous years. One of the main reasons for this is development that has made incursions into the traditional habitat of the monkeys. Their search for food and shelter has presented a major problem for the farming community. This is an example of the challenge that islands face when their small size does not allow for major economic expansion without a significant detrimental impact.

Sustainable development focuses on preserving the environment and promoting social advancement while pursuing economic development. Addressing the challenges presented by the expansion of economic activity into the monkeys' habitat has to be guided by a focus on sustainable development.

I have felt for some time that a possible solution could be the establishment of monkey sanctuaries or sanctuaries that more broadly preserve the wildlife of the islands. This could satisfy many different populations, including tourists, as a new activity could be created for their viewing pleasure; farmers, as they would have an opportunity to produce crops unhindered by the monkeys; and, of course, the monkey and wildlife population would have a safe environment filled with both food and shelter.

When I observed the fire dancers in Samoa, I reflected on the various performances I had seen on islands throughout the world.

On St. Kitts, we have the fire eaters, who dance in a similar fashion, twirling sticks of fire around their bodies. The performance ends when these dancers "eat" the fire, forcing it into their mouths, much to the delight of the audience. In the Bahamas, the limbo dancers also dance under a flame, going lower and lower with each round, while in Fiji, the fire lighting ceremony at the end of the day brings the entire village out to observe.

Samoan fire dancer.

While enjoying these performances, I wondered about the frequency of the performances for the local audiences. Are these performances mainly for the tourists now, or do we, as islanders, continue to enjoy and appreciate them? I reflected on this because I had not recently seen some of the local cultural performances I remembered as a child. Was it because we took local customs for granted and did not support them as we had once done?

Culture connects us to our past, and each performance or presentation helps us to understand our forebears, our fellow islanders, and, invariably, ourselves. Culture is a link that binds the generations.

I understand this now and appreciate even more those who try to preserve island culture.

Samoan police band.

As I stood and listened to the Samoan police band, memories of my cadet days came flooding back. During the Samoa conference, I took note that they played familiar tunes at the parade, which I assume came from our shared Commonwealth past.

As a child, I loved to observe the Remembrance Day parade. The St. Kitts and Nevis Defence Force Band and the various uniformed details marching past always brought a sense of awe to my youthful sensibilities.

When I joined the cadets, it was a form of extracurricular activity for me, and it brought life lessons that became a part of my routine for success.

The cadets helped to reinforce in me a sense of national pride, and being one of those in uniform, marching by as the younger children watched in awe, was gratifying.

Seeing the police band in Samoa, which thrilled onlookers with the precision of its drills, took me back to the camaraderie I felt during those parades, especially when one of the summer camps brought other cadets from the neighboring islands together.

But for me, the cadets also represented one of the opportunities for island youths to explore different ventures that would aid in their growth and character development. Whether it was the sports, the music, the arts, or the debating societies, the personal, community, and national pride remained with those who continued to engage in these pursuits into their adult lives. I am sure that those who represented their islands in one of these ventures still look back fondly on the experience and can attribute some of their later successes to them.

I hope that island youth can continue to have these extracurricular opportunities and options. Financial constraints limit activities, but the benefits to the personal development of future leaders are priceless.

Transportation to an indigenous village in Fiji.

After making it to shore during my trip to an indigenous village in Fiji, I realized that these boats were the main mode of transportation for quite a few of the villagers in the Fijian outer islands. I had mixed emotions, one being the perhaps overly romantic hope that this way of life could be preserved, even with the temptations of the outside world close by, while the other side of that emotional coin concerned my realization that probably a few younger Fijians looked in awe at the outside world, eager to be a part of it all.

The balance is always delicate, but the boat reminded me that those who chose to leave could always find their way back home, eventually.

This picture also resonated with me when I reflected on the story of the students in the Solomon Islands and of my parent's generation in Anguilla, seeking education in St. Kitts as high school students.

Happily, Anguillans are now able to stay on the island for their education, but I know there are other islanders around the world who embark on these journeys across the waters in their pursuit of tutelage, leaving family and loved ones behind. Hopefully, they too will one day be educated close to home.

I am inspired by those islanders who were successful in bringing primary, secondary, and tertiary education to their shores. Perhaps, we can learn from those lessons to ensure that this initiative occurs in many more islands.

MARKETS AROUND THE WORLD

The importance of the marketplace to islanders around the world was not lost on me on these journeys. The goods being sold, mostly island products, have helped to promote local business for many generations.

Markets once represented the pulse of the island communities, bringing agriculture, commerce, and trade opportunities to the family plot, small farmer, and larger enterprises alike.

The interaction in the markets of people from all walks of life helped to maintain islanders' identity as they all connected in these buildings.

Even among the island diaspora, the significance of the market to the community can be seen.

Market in St. Kitts. (Photo courtesy of Marissa Richardson.)

Sir Selwyn Selwyn-Clarke Market, Mahé, the Seychelles.

Market in Fiji.

Dominican market in New York City.

Restaurant sign on 181st Street in Washington Heights, New York.

Walking around 181st Street truly is a walk within the soul of the Dominican Republic. This advertisement promoting a typical Dominican breakfast of plantain, fried cheese, salami—*los tres golpes* (the three hits)—and eggs ensured that the island diaspora remained in sync with the cuisine of their parents as well as their cousins "back home."

It was heartening for me to see the diaspora enjoying and promoting their island cuisine. In recent years, islanders have witnessed robust marketing from outside for non-island foods, and the local products have taken a hit.

I still remember the girl with the apple in primary school, but—at least in that case—it was a healthy alternative. Some of the food coming to the islands is not healthy. Once, when I was in a local supermarket, I observed a sticker on some shipped goods that read, "For Export Only." I wondered, if it was for export only, was something wrong with it? Was it not good enough for the health standards in North America? My suspicious antenna kicked in, but I never knew the reason for the sticker.

I have stayed in some island hotels where I ate food that I could find easily in North America and Europe. As a tourist, I prefer island cuisine, but I probably seek island food because I am an islander. I wonder if tourists from other countries feel the same. Do they like the island cuisine or want more of what they eat at home?

It is important for island cuisine to be appreciated. It can be a healthier option than the imports, and it is definitely very satisfying. I liked the Dominican diaspora's enjoyment of their island cuisine away from home.

THE ARCHITECTURE

The architecture of islands says a lot about the thinking of their people. Each construct, while influenced by external considerations, maintains an island element and tries to take in the nuances of the land and its people.

When you travel throughout the various islands, you can easily sense the psyche of the people, all exhibiting similar world views despite their distance from each other.

Other similarities among the islands can be seen in the historical buildings, which showcase similar architectural designs; the marinas that bring tourists and islanders alike to the waterways; and the religious structures.

While looking at the architecture, I thought about those who designed and built the buildings. Many were built by non-islanders, and sometimes, unfortunately, islanders had no role in the construction.

I remember that during my high school years a multinational hotel chain wanted to construct a five-star hotel in St. Kitts. This would have been the island's first hotel of that level of quality and would have done wonders for our tourism industry. However, the hoteliers had designs on one of the top ecological areas, and rather than accommodating this environment, they wanted to destroy the natural habitat. Many of the local physical planners were horrified. Not only did they understand the value of preserving the environment but they also knew from the topography of the area that the building might eventually sink.

The hoteliers did not listen and proceeded to build. But as fate would have it, the local experts were correct. The structure started sinking, and the hoteliers disappeared to another island.

Islanders bring a different perspective with their innovative ideas, which is also an area that needs to be nurtured and developed among island peoples. If given the opportunity, I know island innovators would create great things that would inspire not just their local communities but the global community as well.

When we look at our architecture, it is more than just beauty and history. For the islands, with their constant rain and sun, architecture must also be about function. You'll find, in looking both at native structures such as the *fale* of Polynesia, with its sloping, tightly woven tops, or even the colonial structures in St. Kitts, with their angled roofs and wrap-around verandas, the climate conditions are always in the mind of the architect. This concept of merging nature and architecture is something islanders can teach the world, no matter the climate conditions.

HISTORICAL HOUSES

Fairview Inn, Colonial House, now a hotel and restaurant in St. Kitts.

House in Samoa.

MARINAS

Marina at Eden Island in the Seychelles.

Marina in Fiji.

CITY CENTERS

Clock in St. Kitts city center. (Photo courtesy of Marissa Richardson.)

Clock tower/war memorial in Apia city center, Samoa.

HINDU TEMPLES

Sri Siva Subramaniya Temple in Nadi, Fiji.

Arul Mihu Navasakthi Vinayagar Temple, Victoria, Mahé, the Seychelles.